JEREMY TAYLOR

BY

EDMUND GOSSE

GREENWOOD PRESS, PUBLISHERS
NEW YORK   1968

PREFATORY NOTE

THIS volume contains a conscientious attempt to present for the first time a detailed biography of Jeremy Taylor. It is remarkable that the career of so eminent and so beloved a writer should not have attracted more attention from literary historians. But its incidents were neglected during the lifetime of those who could have remembered him, and were not made the object of inquiry until external evidence could no longer be obtained. The *Funeral Sermon*, published by George Rust, Bishop of Dromore, in 1668, is a document invaluable to the biographer, but it stands alone. Some particulars were added by Anthony à Wood, and some by Harris in his 1746 edition of the *Works* of Sir James Ware, who, however, died before Jeremy Taylor.

In the eighteenth century several efforts were made to collect notes for Taylor's memoirs, in particular by George Horne, Bishop of Norwich, and then by Thomas Zouch, the antiquary, but these were abandoned for lack of material. In 1793, to a volume of selections, Wheeldon prefixed a Life, which is a mere paraphrase of Rust, and is without independent value.

The Rev. Henry Kaye Bonney was the first to suc-
ceed in making original researches, which he used in
his memoir of Jeremy Taylor published in 1815. This
book, however, is inadequate and untrustworthy, and
no one became more conscious of its defects than
Bonney himself, who set himself to correct it, and
who, when he heard that Heber was engaged in
editing Jeremy Taylor, generously withdrew his book
from circulation, and placed his corrections and fresh
information in Heber's hands.

Every student of Jeremy Taylor owes a debt of
gratitude to Reginald Heber, afterwards Bishop of
Calcutta, for his edition of the text and for his careful commentary. He worked at the former when he
was vicar of Hodnet, Salop, and he finished it just
before he went out to India. The *Works* appeared in
1822, in fifteen volumes, and contained a Life which
threw a flood of new light over the biography and
bibliography of Jeremy Taylor. As was inevitable,
however, in surveying a tract of literary history so
long and so completely neglected, Heber's narrative
contained a large number of misstatements, and he
was moreover the victim of a mystification which will
presently be referred to. His exile in India, and his
premature death, prevented any revision of his valuable work. Meanwhile, J. S. Hughes, in 1831, prefixed
to a selection from Taylor's *Works* a Life that has no
biographical value. But in 1847 the Rev. Robert
Aris Willmott, of Bearwood, published a very graceful

little book entitled *Bishop Jeremy Taylor, his Prede-cessors, Contemporaries, and Successors*, a sketch of the English Church in the seventeenth century, in the course of which he corrected Heber in some par-ticulars, and added one or two fresh facts.

All these biographies were superseded, however, by the labours of the Rev. Charles Page Eden, fellow of Oriel, and vicar of St. Mary's, Oxford, who undertook the complete revision of Heber's *Jeremy Taylor*. His edition of the *Works*, which was in ten volumes, and occupied several years, was completed in 1854 by what was called volume i., which contained Heber's Life of Jeremy Taylor, corrected, enlarged, and sup-plied with voluminous notes. Eden was a fine scholar, and he must have been one of the most modest of men, for he concealed the importance of his work under the guise of a loyal fidelity to Heber. He is, therefore, scarcely named by the bibliographers, yet it is no more than justice to point out that it is his recension of Heber's memoir, very inconveniently arranged, indeed, being cumbered with notes and appendices, and hidden away in the midst of other editorial matter, which forms the only authoritative biography of Jeremy Taylor.

Since Eden's day, no Life of Taylor has been issued which can be named as having any independent value. For the collection of documents and quotation of authorities, his still remains the one entirely indis-pensable publication dealing with the career of the

Bishop. But, in the course of the fifty years which
have elapsed since Eden put down his pen, the history
of the seventeenth century has been greatly elucidated.
At various points his narrative needs to be enlarged
and corrected in detail, and it is with no sentiment
but one of gratitude to Eden, and admiration of his
scholarship, that the writer of this volume feels that
the time has arrived for a more minute and a more
consecutive biography of Jeremy Taylor. In particular, the labour of Ulster church antiquaries has
discovered, and has published in various fugitive
forms, a great deal about the Bishop's Irish experiences which could not be known to Heber or to Eden.
These have been well used in the short summary of
Taylor's life, contributed by the Rev. T. B. Johnstone
to the *Dictionary of National Biography*.

It is necessary, however, to speak of an element in
the biography of Jeremy Taylor which has hitherto
been accepted in every account of his life, and which
I have slowly and reluctantly been obliged to reject.
When Heber was collecting material for the 1822
edition, he was favoured with some manuscripts which
he described as "among the most interesting hitherto
recovered concerning Bishop Taylor's private concerns." They purported to be the papers of William
Todd Jones of Homra, who had been occupied all his
life, so it was averred, in collecting documents for
a biography of Jeremy Taylor, from whom he was
lineally descended "in the fifth degree." Mr. Jones

died suddenly, in 1818, by being thrown out of his carriage, when all his notes and manuscripts were found to have absolutely vanished. In a mysterious way, however, some of them, and particularly reminiscences said to have been contained in a letter written in 1732 by a Lady Wray, said to have been a granddaughter of Jeremy Taylor, were eventually placed in Heber's hands. Heber did not print them verbatim, probably because he saw that in many particulars it was impossible that they could be correct. Many of the statements which he did pass were quietly expunged later on by Eden, who evidently could not tell what to make of Lady Wray. But many more have hitherto been repeated, until they form part of Taylor's accepted biography.

In very careful examination of what remains of Lady Wray's reminiscences, I have gradually come to the startling conclusion that they are apocryphal, and my narrative is accordingly deprived of some romantic but ridiculous incidents. In one or two cases I have shown the accepted story to be preposterous; in others I have simply dropped it out of the record. This is not the place to examine the whole of this curious and disconcerting business of Lady Wray's pretended traditions, but I hope elsewhere to do so in detail. I have no doubt left in my own mind that the whole thing was a mystification or hoax, by which Heber was deceived. The probable origin of this strange fraud it is perhaps too late to conjecture, and it is always

possible that the letter of May 31, 1732, may have
existed, and may even have been written in good faith,
though in that case with a recklessness of ignorance
positively amazing.   For practical purposes, it is time
that it should cease to be quoted among authorities
for the biography of Jeremy Taylor.

                                              E. G.

   October, 1903.

CONTENTS

JEREMY TAYLOR

CHAPTER I

CHILDHOOD AND YOUTH

(1613–1642)

REGARDING the ancestry of Jeremy Taylor much has
been conjectured but little is known. During the
seventeenth century no suggestion was made that his
parentage had been other than obscure and simple.
But in 1732 his granddaughter, Lady Wray, is supposed to have stated that the family held a respectable
rank among the smaller gentry of Gloucestershire,
"where they had possessed for many generations an
estate in the parish of Frampton-on-Severn." There
has been no confirmation of this statement; but another
pretension of Lady Wray's has proved irresistible by all
Jeremy Taylor's biographers, although close examination shows it no less devoid of basis. She said that
Nathaniel Taylor, the father of the bishop, "was the
lineal descendant of Dr. Rowland Taylor," the martyr.
This is so delightful a supposition that no one has
opposed it; and Heber even found "a filial fondness"
in the way in which Jeremy speaks of Rowland in *An
Apology for Liturgy*. He praises him enthusiastically,
it is true, but it would be hard if we were supposed to

claim kinship with all of whom we write in terms of admiration.

If Nathaniel Taylor was "the lineal descendant" of Cranmer's famous chaplain, who was burned at the stake, by Bonner's command, in 1555, he could only have been his grandson, and Edmund Taylor, the churchwarden, must have been one of Rowland Taylor's four surviving children. But if the relationship was so close — and dates forbid our making it more remote — how are we to explain the fact that in the discreet Cambridge household, where three generations worked humbly side by side, the glory of descending so recently and directly from a prominent local celebrity was not sedulously claimed? We may, I am afraid, depend upon it that if Jeremy Taylor had been the great-grandson of the martyr, it would not have been left to Lady Wray to be the first to inform us. But Taylor himself seems to lay a vague claim to gentility. He used a seal with the arms " Ermine, on a chief, indented, sable, three escallops, or : the crest a lion rampant, issuant, ermine, having between his paws a ducal coronet, or " : these are also engraved on his portraits. This is the coat confirmed to a certain Roger Taylor, in 1614, but by what right the bishop assumed it, if he did so, remains quite unknown. In 1651 he asked Dugdale for information about this coat of arms, but we know not what reply the antiquary made. Where conjectures are so prevalent, I wonder that no one has sought to find a tie between the barber's son and the eminent Dr. Thomas Taylor, who was standing "as a brazen wall against popery," and teaching Hebrew at Christ's College, within a stone's-throw of Nathaniel Taylor's shop, all through the boyhood of Jeremy.

When gifts and graces abound so signally as they did in the person of the Bishop of Down and Connor, it is only human to suppose that they must be inherited.

JEREMY TAYLOR sprang from a respectable Cambridge family of the lower middle class. His grandfather, Edmund Taylor, had been churchwarden of the parish of Trinity, certainly since 1589. The churchwarden's son Nathaniel married Mary Dean in 1605, and they had six children, of whom the subject of this memoir was the fourth child, and the third son. According to tradition, the house in which the Taylors lived was that later known as the Black Bull,[1] opposite Trinity Church, and here doubtless Jeremy Taylor was born. About the date of this event an uncertainty rests. He was baptized on the 15th of August 1613, but it was found to have been suggested by his Irish contemporary, Sir James Ware, in his posthumous papers, that Taylor was, really, at least two years old at the time. The immediate reason for such a supposition will presently appear; but it must be said at once that to accept it would be to dislocate the whole record of Jeremy's brothers and sister, who appear on the registers at regular intervals of two years. From earliest infancy the future bishop seems to have been singularly precocious. His father, Nathaniel Taylor, was a barber by trade. There is no evidence that he belonged to the higher grade of barber-surgeon; but

[1] In his *Virgidemiarum* of 1597, where Joseph Hall celebrates twelve leading hostelries of Cambridge as symbolical of the signs of the Zodiac, he includes the Black Bull and the Wrestlers, both afterwards identified with Jeremy Taylor. This may be the "creeping into every blind taphouse," for which Milton reproves Hall.

he was a man of education, and the son was " solely
grounded in grammar and mathematics " by his father.

Early in the childhood of Jeremy Taylor, Dr. Stephen
Perse, a fellow and bursar of Caius College, who had
large landed property in Cambridge, died, leaving a
will by which his town and college were generously
benefited.   Among other charges, his executors were
directed to buy certain grounds and tenements on
which to erect a convenient free grammar school for
the use of a hundred scholars.   The original Perse
School, which existed until about sixty years ago, and
stood in what was called Luthburne Lane, where the
Cavendish Laboratory now stands, was finished and
opened in 1619, and its first master was Thomas Lover-
ing, a graduate of Pembroke College.   Hither, and to the
teaching of this excellent master, who was said to make
learning so attractive to his pupils that they became
" Minerva's darlings," Jeremy Taylor passed at the age
of six; he was probably one of the original scholars
when the grammar school was opened.   About 1621
the barber and his family moved to a house afterwards
known as the Wrestlers' Inn, in Petty Cury, a few
doors from their earlier home, and a little nearer the
Perse School.

Jeremy Taylor spent seven years at school, and then
proceeded to Gonville and Caius College, where he was
admitted as a sizar on the 18th of August 1626.   Here
we are confronted with a puzzle, for the admission-
book states that he was at the time in the fifteenth
year of his age.   As a fact he could but very recently
have entered his fourteenth.   The book goes on to
prove itself of slight authority in the matter of dates,
by saying that Jeremy had attended the Perse School

for some ten years, whereas that institution had been
in existence for no more than seven. We may disregard these erroneous entries, merely noticing that
the rumour of Taylor's being older than he supposed
is doubtless founded upon them, and upon the miracle
of his precocious scholarship, for he was ripe for the
university before custom would allow of his admittance.
Rust, his faithful friend and earliest biographer, cor-
rectly records that he entered college as soon as he was
thirteen years of age.

In leaving school, Jeremy Taylor did not deprive
himself of the patronage of Stephen Perse. There had
of late years been a great expansion of the University
of Cambridge and a corresponding lack of accommodation. By his admirable will, Dr. Perse relieved that
pressure so far as his own college was concerned, by
founding six fellowships and six scholarships, and by
leaving money to build lodgings and chambers for the
holders of these, and for many other persons. In 1617
the Perse buildings rose on the north side of the
entrance-court of the college, on ground which Perse
had bought from Trinity. The beautiful symbolism
of the gates of Caius — which was destroyed and
rendered absurd by the manipulations of 1869 — was
still in full force. When Jeremy Taylor came from
the barber's shop in Petty Cury, across the Market
Place and by St. Mary's, he would enter, as a youthful
s′ ar should, at the Gate of Humility (which then
opened into what is now Trinity Street, opposite St.
Michael's Church), and would turn to the right across
Brick Court. The building, which was his home from
1626 until 1635, was one of the most agreeable in the
university. Dr. Perse's bequest had been ample, and

the new chambers were roomy and convenient. There
were two stories, containing sets of studies, and oaken
staircases led up to a third story of garrets or, as they
were called, " excelses." The chambers looked out on
St. Michael's Lane in front; at the back, across Brick
Court, to the Gonville buildings and to the chapel,
which was being enlarged just when Jeremy Taylor
finally left college. On either side the light fell
through casements, provided with good Burgundy
glass in small, well-soldered lozenges. All was comfortable, in the simple sense of the time; even the
excelses, in one of which Taylor doubtless found his
first lodging, were well equipped.

Of the nine years which the future bishop spent at
college we know little. Within the local circle his
grace and tact and earnestness won the admiration of
his companions. We are told that the impression he
produced was such that "had he lived among the
ancient pagans he had been ushered into the world
with a miracle, and swans must have danced and sung
at his birth." He was " a great hero " in the ranks of
college scholarship, and was looked upon as "no less
than the son of Apollo, the god of wisdom and eloquence." His tutor was Thomas Batchcroft, a strong
royalist, who became Master of the college, and was
ultimately ejected by the Parliamentarians. To his
teaching we may attribute Taylor's earliest leanings
to the king's cause. The boy's progress was steady and
rapid: he matriculated on the 17th of March 1627,
was elected a Perse scholar at Michaelmas of the following year, took his degree early in his eighteenth
year, and was elected a Perse fellow at the age of
twenty. He was a man, Rust tells us, long before he

was of age, and had known "of the state of childhood little more than its innocency and pleasantness."

In the course of his *Liberty of Prophesying*, Jeremy Taylor remarked, twelve years after he left college, that "education is so great and so invincible a prejudice, that he who masters the inconvenience of it is more to be commended than he can justly be blamed that complies with it." His own career was a comment on this passage. No one was ever more inconvenienced than he by the prejudice of that education which he received at Cambridge, and few have tried more manfully to master it. But the very narrow circle of minds among whom he was trained at college were filled with the passion of prerogative government in Church and State, and the duty of upholding it by all the apparatus of applied patristic literature. In a less intellectual and more physical sense, the laborious youth of Taylor presents itself to us as repressed within such limits as are now not endurable by an agricultural labourer. From the barber's shop in Petty Cury to the Perse School, thence to Caius College, and thence back to the shop, this is a round which can be calmly made in fifteen minutes, yet it comprises all we know of the first twenty years of the life of Jeremy Taylor. During the greater part of his college career, Milton, George Herbert, Fuller, Crashaw, and Henry More were inmates of the same university. Jeremy Taylor may well have brushed against the sleeves of each of them as he passed along the narrow streets of Cambridge. But not one of their lives touched his; not one thought of theirs diverted him for a moment from his solitary course of study.

An accident broke up the stillness of Taylor's sequestered life, and flung him into the world. In 1633, being below the canonical age, he took holy orders, and in 1634 became a master of arts. His chamber-fellow (the usual arrangement was that two graduates slept in large beds in the outer chamber of each set of rooms, in the company of two scholars in smaller beds, which in the daytime were pushed out of sight below the larger), a Rev. Thomas Risden, three years his senior, was engaged as a preacher at St. Paul's. Being prevented from carrying out his duties, Risden persuaded Jeremy Taylor to go up to London and preach in his place. It is evident that the younger man must already, perhaps in the college chapel, have proved his aptitude for public speaking, since at Michaelmas 1634 he was appointed by the Master to be prælector in rhetoric. At all events, he proceeded to St. Paul's in Risden's place and preached on suc-cessive occasions " to the admiration and astonishment of his auditory." His success was instantaneous, and his sermons the sensation of the moment ; it became the fashion to go to hear this young Mr. Taylor from Cambridge. We are told that "by his florid and youthful beauty, and sweet and pleasant air, and sub-lime and raised discourses, he made his hearers take him for some young angel, newly descended from the visions of glory." No one had preached in this way since the divine Dr. Donne, occupant of that very pul-pit, had died three years before.

We have in all probability reached the autumn of 1634, and the opening of Jeremy Taylor's twenty-second year. He had now the fatal fortune of attracting the favour of the most powerful and the most unlucky man in England. The fame of the new star, that

already "outshone" all the rest of the ecclesiastical
firmament, came to the ears of Laud, and Jeremy
Taylor was commanded to preach before his Grace.
If Laud had questioned the reports which had reached
him, he doubted no longer. He frankly recognised the
genius of the astonishing youth with wonder and satisfaction. Among all Laud's faults, a disdain of learning
and subtlety has never been enumerated; he set himself at once to draw music from an instrument so delicate and rich, and already attuned so carefully to the
note of prerogative. This was a critical time in Laud's
career; since August 1633 he had been Primate of
England, and the threads of the whole ecclesiastical
system were in his hand. He was at length enabled
by vigorous administration of the ecclesiastical law
to treat the extreme section of the Puritans with
unmitigated severity. He was drawing the cords of
discipline with more and more angry impatience
around every limb of the unfortunate English Church,
and those who resisted him had to flee, as best they
might, to Holland, to Maryland, or to Massachusetts.

For the next two years we know nothing of the
fortunes of Jeremy Taylor, except that he lived under
the protection and guidance of Laud. Rust has preserved a pleasant anecdote of the youth's early conversation with his patron. The archbishop, after
hearing him preach, very graciously admitted that his
"discourse was beyond exception," and even "beyond
imitation." But "the wise prelate thought him too
young," and indeed twenty-two years is but a modest
age for a divine. Jeremy Taylor proved his wit, and,
if we consider the circumstances, his courage, by replying that he humbly begged his Grace to pardon that

fault of youth, and promised "if he lived he would mend it." It is certain that Laud was greatly pleased with him, and there is no reason to believe that his favour ever flagged. It has been often said that Laud could not appreciate geniality in others, yet he recognised it in Juxon and in Taylor. Perhaps it would be safer to say, that he neither appreciated it nor heeded it in those whose views in any measure differed from his own, but it seems as though he recognised the importance of graceful manners in men who were zealously employed in his work.

This year, 1635, marked the height of Laud's success. Without imagination or the power of looking forward, ignorant of the mainsprings of human action, led on by the desire to do what in his contracted earnestness he deemed to be right, at whatever cost to himself or others, the abyss was already opening before him. But he had little conception of it. He thought that he was conquering all along the line of opposition, warding off Rome on the one hand, crushing Puritan nonconformity on the other. In the glorious task he had set himself, he needed aiders and abettors. He could not begin too early to train labourers for his vineyard. Fresh Juxons and Wrens and Montagus must be trained to carry on the irresistible policy of Thorough; where there was any splendour of talent and virtue in the English Church it must be captured young, and be shielded from caprice. Two years were to pass before it was brought home to that stubborn and rigorous nature that he might fail in his purpose, and might drag down in his fall those institutions of monarchy and Episcopacy which he loved so sincerely.

Meanwhile the juvenile Jeremy Taylor was but one,

even if the most brilliantly gifted, of the youthful
divines of promise whom it was the archbishop's duty
to train for the work of repression and reform.   We
do not know whether Laud permitted him to return
to Cambridge, or whether he brought him to London;
Taylor did not vacate his fellowship at Caius College
until Lady Day 1636.   Laud's admiration of the young
man's genius did not blind him to his immaturity; and
the "young angel, newly descended from the visions
of glory," required careful training in the more mundane and instant parts of ecclesiastical discipline.   To
the prosaic mind of Laud, it is not at all certain that
the ecstatic dream, the coloured reverie of Taylor,
would greatly appeal.   He would admire it, no doubt,
and love the holy and charming young proficient, but
he would see a danger in it.   The great thing was the
cause of Thorough.   In this was Taylor sound ?

The answer to this question must be that, so far as
we can discern, Taylor was absolutely sound.   He had
none of the spirit of a revolutionary; his nature, rev-
erential and timid, accepted the authority before him
without question.   It is not impossible that the archbishop took Taylor with him on those metropolitan
visitations which he had lately started.   It is certain
that he found him, at present, too rhetorical and
imaginative for his practical purposes, and decided, in
language which betrayed an affectionate pride in so
candid and docile a disciple, that it was " for the advantage of the world, that such mighty parts should
be afforded better opportunities of study and improvement than a course of constant preaching would allow
of "; he determined that Taylor should settle at
Oxford.   It has been thought surprising, and compli-

mentary neither to the learning nor the loyalty of
Cambridge, that Laud should have chosen for this
purpose the other university.   But this shows a failure
to comprehend the special meaning attached by the
archbishop to "study and improvement."   What
Laud designed was that Taylor should enter the circle
at Oxford which was being carefully prepared as
a forcing-house for the ideas which alone seemed
salutary to his bitter pertinacity of purpose.

So completely had one society in Oxford become
the centre of Laud's system of *propaganda*, that Rust
actually says that at this juncture the archbishop
placed Jeremy Taylor "in his own college of All Souls
in Oxford," although, of course, in the exact and usual
sense, Laud was not even a member of that college.
On the 23rd of October 1635, he wrote from Lambeth
to the Warden and Fellows of All Souls recommending
to them "Mr. Jeremiah Taylor," as "an honest man
and a good scholar," and heartily praying that he
should be elected to the fellowship left vacant by the
enforced retirement of a Mr. Osborne, for whom Laud
provided elsewhere.   It appears from the archbishop's
letter, that Taylor had already been incorporated into
Oxford, with an *ad eundem* degree, at University
College.   Laud writes in his customary dictatorial
tone, and it is certain that formal difficulties presented
themselves, Gilbert Sheldon, the Warden of All Souls,
afterwards Archbishop of Canterbury, protesting
against the high-handed procedure of Laud in this
delicate matter.   Jeremy Taylor, however, after a
hurried and probably final visit to Cambridge, presented
himself at Oxford, and was inspected by the fellows of
All Souls.   They fell under his irresistible charm, and

pronounced him "a person of most wonderful parts, and like to be an ornament" to their society. The formal difficulty was avoided by holding no election, but Laud, in his right as visitor of the college, nominated his protégé to the vacant probationary fellowship at All Souls on the 3rd of November 1635, the society being "almost unanimous" in welcoming him. On the 14th of January 1636, he was admitted a "true and perpetual fellow" of the college.

Here, then, for two years we have to think of him, sedately preparing for the work which seemed to lie before him, and learning, as Anthony à Wood says, what would "enable him to write casuistically." His native eloquence and fancy were checked during this period of preparation in the school of Thorough. It was another *Appello Cæsarem* that his impetuous patron wished him to produce, and not a *Holy Dying* or a *Great Exemplar*. Laud took care not to lose sight of him; he made the young divine his chaplain, and doubtless often summoned him to Lambeth, that he might observe the growth of his mind and strengthen his resolution.

Several interesting men are known to have come into contact with Jeremy Taylor during his early years at Oxford. His intimacy with Franciscus à Sancta Clara was close, and the memory of it developed after his departure into an Oxford legend. Sancta Clara, whose real name was Christopher Davenport, a man of many pseudonyms, was a missionary friar, who had lately arrived from Douai. He was a subtle and highly adroit personage, whose aim in life was to reconcile the English Church with Rome, and to do so by the gentlest and most insinuating of flatteries. He

conciliated society with success; the king became more
than tolerant to Sancta Clara; the queen took him as
her chaplain; he grew intimate with many of the
Anglican bishops, and Laud himself was afterwards
accused by the Puritans of encouraging him. In
slightly later years than we have yet reached, the
graceful Franciscan pervaded Oxford, carrying with
him a purpose of courtly casuistry and insidious en-
croachment. That he paid particular attention to the
youthful fellow of All Souls, and was careful to cultivate his conversation, was a proof of the signal promise
already given by the nature of Jeremy Taylor.

A more interesting acquaintance offered itself to
Taylor at Oxford. On arriving there, he found the
university animated by the presence of a spirit of
wonderful brightness, and a conscience personally dis-
interested to a rare degree, but fretful, litigious, and
violently swayed by every wind of doctrine. This was
the extraordinary William Chillingworth, Laud's god-
son, who had gone over to Rome, and had actually
retired for a time to the Jesuits' college in Douai, but
who, in 1631, had been turned again, by Laud's correspondence, from "a doubting Papist into a confirmed
Protestant." A wavering and sceptical judgment, re-
lentlessly lighted by what was doubtless the acutest intellect at that time applied in England to ecclesiastical
matters, Chillingworth's love of dialectic for its own
sake was so pronounced, that it was a jest in Oxford
that he might be seen hurrying up and down in Trinity
Garden, searching for somebody to dispute with. Thus
Chillingworth had gone in and out, seeking rest and
finding none. Laud, who admired him, and humoured
him with signal patience, was doubtless pleased that

his younger and more docile friend should sharpen
his wits against the keenest intelligence in Oxford.
And by 1636, Chillingworth was already partly calm-
ing himself in the preparation of his own great and
famous book.   •

We have an interesting glimpse of Taylor in one
of Chillingworth's letters of this time, written during
an absence from Oxford in which he begs his correspondent, or Mr. (afterwards Sir Henry) Coventry, to
tell Jeremy Taylor that " one that knows him " — that
is Chillingworth himself — has been heard to " magnify
him exceedingly for other things, but censure him for "
one, namely his inattention to the reasonings of others.
This keen observer, who had been greatly impressed
by the young divine's ability, was nevertheless struck
by his neglect of the arguments of his opponent;
" methinks," says Chillingworth, " he wants much of
the ethical part of a discourser, and slights too much
many times the arguments of those he discourses with."
Taylor was, in fact, far more of a rhetorician than of a
casuist, just as in later years he was to be rather a
religious man of letters than a logical theologian.   But
the terms of Chillingworth's letter, in which he begs
his friend to delay his admonition long enough to
prevent Taylor from suspecting who his critic is, and
to be candid with the utmost gentleness, prove the
high affection and esteem which Taylor inspired.   At
his own college, we are told, " love and admiration still
waited upon him," and the appreciation of his " extraordinary worth and sweetness " was universal.   No
doubt, had Chillingworth spoken directly to Taylor
about his want of interest in argument, his young
friend would gently and gaily have returned the parry.

We know that the dialectic of Oxford churchmen
seemed dry enough to him in later years, as he looked
back with a smile to the days when he listened to
" persons of great understanding oftentimes so amused
with the authority of their church, that it is pity to
see them sweat in answering some objections, which
they know not how to do, but yet believe they must,
because the church hath said it." A description of
Chillingworth, too, seems to have hitherto escaped
notice in the labyrinths of Taylor's *Ductor Dubitantium :* " I knew a scholar once who was a man of a
quick apprehension, and easy to receive an objection,
who when he read the Roman doctors was very much
of their opinion, and as much against them when he
read their adversaries ; but kept himself to the religion
of his country, concerning which at all times he remembered that there were rare arguments and answers
respectively, though he could not then think upon
them."

With his twenty-fifth year, Taylor's period of pro-
bation came to a close. Laud was satisfied with the
success of his experiment, and gave the faithful disciple his first rewards. The year 1638 was critical
in Taylor's career. Laud determined on one of those
complex shiftings by which he encouraged his followers, and was vigilant in pulling up those weeds of
Puritan disaffection which the soil of England was now
" too apt to nourish." The valuable incumbency of Uppingham, in Rutlandshire, had been held since 1631 by
Dr. Edward Martin, President of Queens' College, and
one of Laud's most faithful supporters at Cambridge,
ultimately Dean of Ely. Martin never resided at
Uppingham, where the duty was performed by his

curate, Peter Hausted, a small dramatist of some note, author of *The Rival Friends*. Laud, acting in the name of Juxon, who, now that he was Lord High Treasurer, left these questions of minor preferment to his friend and chief, transferred Martin to another rich sinecure, that of Houghton Conquest, in Bedfordshire, and on the 23rd of March 1638 instituted Jeremy Taylor to Uppingham. Taylor was not inclined to leave his duties to be performed by a curate, and Peter Hausted, who had proved himself a zealous High Churchman, was made rector of Much Hadham in Herts; he died a little later, in the dark year 1645, fighting at the siege of Banbury.

Taylor made Uppingham his principal place of residence for about four years, during which time the entries in the parish books testify to the zeal with which he carried out his duties as rector. The quiet of the country life, far from the wordy contests of Oxford, was a great consolation to his spirit. He was now, for the first time, able to cultivate the things that he loved best, the reading of the Scriptures, and the methods by which the contemplative spirit can suck most sweetness from that honeycomb, namely, as he says himself, industry, meditation, conference, the human arts and sciences, and whatever " God and good news " offer as a reward for intellectual service. Of Taylor's experiences at Uppingham we know very little; doubtless there was not much in his sequestered habits to record. One little vignette we possess, like a peep through the chink of a door. Mrs. Edward Turner of Little Dalby, though a parson's wife, was on her road to Rome, when she consulted Jeremy Taylor at Uppingham. He took her into his

c

study, and " did enjoin 'her penance " ; when she saw,
and in spite of her tendencies was shocked at the sight,
a little altar with a crucifix upon it. The anecdote
probably dates from about 1640.

The conjectures of the scandalised Mrs. Turner
must be taken for what they are worth, but it seems
certain that about this time Jeremy Taylor, like so
many of the partisans of Thorough, like their tremen-
dous leader himself, was suspected of a tendency to
Popery. It was difficult to hold the straight high
path between the zealots and Rome. The very stiffen-
ing against Puritans made the English priest naturally lean towards ritual, until, as the egregious John
Bastwick said, in 1637, the Church became " as full of
ceremonies as a dog is full of fleas."

Taylor's main intellectual centre was still at Oxford,
where on the 5th of November 1638 he was appointed
to preach at St. Mary's before the University on the
anniversary of Guy Fawkes's Day. Wood gives an
account, evidently by hearsay, of the circumstances
which attended the delivery of this sermon. If we
are to believe him, Taylor had no free hand in the
composition of his address, which the vice-chancellor
first commanded him to prepare, and then enlarged
with many passages of his own, offensive to the Roman
Catholics, so that after preaching it Taylor had to
apologise to his Roman friends, and express his regret
at the opinions which had been put into his mouth.
Wood's authority for some of these statements was
Sancta Clara, who told him that Jeremy Taylor had
" several times expressed some sorrow for those things
he had said." The subtle Franciscan was not to be
trusted, and if Wood had heard Taylor's sermon, or

had read it, he would hardly have repeated these remarks. The whole address bears the mark of one mind and one voice. There is every probability, indeed, that the gracious divine, meeting his Roman acquaintances in Oxford, and being reproached with his attack on them, would cautiously deprecate the idea of any personal unfriendliness. Further than this it is impossible that he could go. The terms in which he afterwards assures us that at no moment of his life was he tempted to acquiesce in the Roman doctrine are too explicit to be overlooked.

The *Sermon on Gunpowder Treason* is the earliest composition of Taylor's which we possess. It is not a sermon in the modern sense, but a dissertation on a point of ecclesiastical law casuistically treated; something, we may say, between a lecture by the Dixie Professor and a Hulsean Lecture. It is dedicated, in a strain of excessive modesty, to Laud; and the preacher states that the Vice-Chancellor had commanded "a publication of these very short and sudden meditations." He speaks as one whose arguments against Rome had long attracted the notice of the authorities, until the university had been drawn to appoint him its "public voice" in a discovery of the king's religious enemies as well as in its "thanksgiving" to Laud himself. So far from attacking the Romanists, the author expresses a lively wish not to seem uncharitable, and, indeed, it is hard to tell how Sancta Clara, or Panzani himself, could reasonably object to a word in the dissertation. The *Sermon on Gunpowder Treason* is not doctrinal: it is entirely directed to one legal point, the assumed right of rebellion against heretical princes; and the Jesuits at Oxford would have been crazy to complain of an official Anglican divine for resisting this particular assumption of theirs.

The style of this address is dry and crabbed, with that incessant quotation from Latin authorities which was at that time so dangerous a vice of English prose. In only a single instance does it rise above the common-place level of the ecclesiastical jurisprudence of the hour. Near the close we find one paragraph which prophesies of the coming greatness of the writer : —

"Now after such a sublimity of malice, I will not instance in the sacrilegious ruin of the neighbouring temples, which needs must have perished in the flame, nor in the disturbing the ashes of our entombed kings, devouring their dead ruins like sepulchral dogs. These are but minutes, in respect of the ruin prepared for the living temples."

These are clumsy phrases and halting cadences, but here we see at least, trying his undeveloped wings, the cygnet that was to become so proud and magnificent a swan.

Jeremy Taylor was now settled in a rising fame as well as fortune; assured of the favour of the party in power, he had a right to expect rapid and high promotion. He proceeded to form for himself a family. Towards the end of his tutorial work at Caius College, he had taught a medical student, Edward Langsdale, the son of a London gentleman. There was great sympathy between the teacher and the pupil, who was but six years his junior, and the relation ripened into a lifelong friendship. Edward Langsdale, who outlived the bishop, became a physician at Gains-borough, and on the 27th of May 1639 Jeremy Taylor married his sister, Phœbe, at Uppingham. Of Phœbe Taylor we know nothing, save that she bore her husband

six (if not seven) children, and that she died during the
time of their retirement in Wales; a son, William,
having died at Uppingham in May 1642. There has
been useless speculation as to the reason of Phœbe
Taylor's obscurity, but she was doubtless a simple
and house-abiding matron of whom there would be
little to record and no one to retail it. Jeremy Taylor
was somewhat reserved under his sweetness. We
know, from *An Apology for Liturgy*, that he did not
love to discuss his household affairs; he was one of
those who "will be so desirous of their liberty as to
preserve that in private, when they have no concern-
ments but their own, for matter of order or scandal."
Such faint indications as we possess point to an un-
ruffled domestic felicity.

Four years now pass in which we are unable to
catch a glimpse of Taylor further than what the formal
registers of Uppingham and All Souls College have to
offer us. In his parish work he was "a rare conductor
of souls, and knew how to counsel and to advise, to
solve difficulties, and determine cares, and quiet consciences." In all this pleasant labour he was certainly
happier than in exercising the casuistry which his visits
to Oxford forced upon him. Nor did he spare his
too passionate colleagues the lambency of his humour,
comparing "their subtilties and spinosities" to the
feats of Don Quixote. He "would make sport sometimes with the romantic sophistry and fantastic adventures of school-errantry." It seems that he was slow
to perceive the gathering storm of cloud. But when
his great patron and the mainstay of his fortunes fell,
he must have been stricken with alarm. In February
1641 Laud was impeached by Sir Harry Vane; on the

1st of March he was sent to the Tower; on the 25th
of June he ceased to be Chancellor of Oxford. A
little later all his rents and profits as Primate were
sequestered. These were fatal dates in the career of
Jeremy Taylor. "I am robbed of that which once did
bless me," he wrote, and all the house of his hopes
must have come crashing about his head.

It does not appear that he had hitherto recognised
in the Puritans a serious danger. He had paid them
little attention; his thoughts and arguments had been
centred on the advances of Rome. No doubt he considered that Laud and Juxon were perfectly well able
to keep the "sectaries" in order. But against the
policy of Thorough had arisen that of Root-and-Branch,
and the harshness of the bishops had brought about its
equally violent reaction. It was probably not until
1641 that Taylor realised that the discipline of Juxon
and the authority of Laud had been strained beyond
bearing, and that, in fact, they were going to be
borne no longer. The scheme of church-government,
in implicit obedience to which the whole of Taylor's
placid youth had been spent, suddenly passed from
the offensive to the defensive attitude. He could
disregard the Puritan advance no longer; he had to
join his brethren in resisting its obtrusive energy,
step by step. For that great contention was now to
be fought out to a definite issue, which the wise poet,
Samuel Daniel, had foreseen so long before, when he
wrote, in his *Musophilus*: —

> "Sacred Religion, mother of form and fear,
>   How gorgeously sometimes dost thou sit decked !
> What pompous vestures do we make thee wear !
>   What stately piles we, prodigal, erect !

How sweet perfum'd thou art !   How shining clear !
   How solemnly observ'd, with what respect !

Another time, all plain, all quite threadbare,
   Thou must have all within, and nought without;
Sit poorly without light, disrob'd, no care
   Of outward grace to amuse the poor devout;
Powerless, unhallowed, scarcely men can spare
   The necessary rites to set thee out.''

CHAPTER II

(1642–1649)

AT the breaking out of the Civil War, in the summer of 1642, Jeremy Taylor's name ceases to appear in the registers of Uppingham, nor does it recur there later. He was now chaplain-in-ordinary to the king, and in all probability he joined the troops when the standard was raised close by him, at Nottingham (August 22). The rectory at Uppingham doubtless continued for some twelve months more to be occupied by his family, since it was their legal home, and there was no species of personal danger imminent to them there. Moreover, no attempt was made to sequester the living until May 1644. Charles I. left Nottingham for Shrewsbury in September, and then proceeded in a south-eastern line direct for Oxford, which, after the indecisive engagement at Edgehill, he reached at the end of October. We may be certain that whether Jeremy Taylor accompanied the king on the campaign, or awaited his arrival at Oxford, he took part in that delusive and ironic triumphal entry "amidst the plaudits of citizens and scholars," which closed the prologue to the long Civil War.

A new patron now arose, to take the place of the

24

fallen Laud. Amongst those who joined Charles I. at
Oxford in November 1642 was Sir Christopher Hatton,
a cousin of the great Chancellor. This gentleman had
possibly been acquainted with Jeremy Taylor at Cambridge, since he was at Jesus College during some of
the years which Taylor spent at Caius. Still more
probably, he had known him as a neighbour, for
Hatton's residence, Kirby Hall, although on the
borders of Rockingham Forest in Northamptonshire,
was but a few miles from Uppingham. Hatton enjoyed
at this time "a great reputation," as Clarendon himself, who disliked him, had to admit. He was considered a person of high judgment, and he imposed
himself upon Charles I., who frequently deferred to
his opinion, and showed him constant favour. For
a moment, Hatton seemed about to become a very
prominent personage in England, but he did not stand
the trial of adversity. " In a few years, he found a
way utterly to lose " the reputation he had made, and
in his old age he was discredited and obscure. But
at the outbreak of the war, he made a brilliant
appearance, and the very best fact that history has
preserved about him is that for six or seven years
he was a liberal patron and faithful friend to Jeremy
Taylor.

The king's chaplain was by this time in the thick
of the intellectual battle. On the 7th of September
the House of Commons had passed a resolution for the
abolition of all bishops, and the Lords had ratified the
motion. It was necessary to contend immediately with
this policy, so violent and monstrous to the consciences
of half of the king's subjects. Jeremy Taylor sat
down to produce that work of his which is commonly

known as *Episcopacy Asserted*, the actual title of which,
as published late in 1642, is *Of the Sacred Order of
Episcopacy*. In this, Taylor's second book, the student
of literature discovers little advance in style. The
excessive use of Latin and Greek quotation continues;
from the brief, clear, argumentative statement all
rhetoric and all ornament are excluded. The book is
more a paraphrase of authorities and a compendium of
ruling cases than a specimen of independent authorship. The original edition of *Episcopacy Asserted* was
dedicated to Hatton in a prefatory discourse, in which
Taylor distinctly says that the statesman is his only
resource; "I am forced upon you." He has found
out that he has no private advantage to expect from
his chaplaincy to the king; "my person must not go
thither to sanctuary unless it be to pay my devotion."
It is to Hatton that the book is commended, as a
"tried friend"; it is Hatton who must be to its
author "a refuge for my need."

The attitude of the young casuist is one of surprised
indignation at the presumption of the sectaries. He
cannot believe that the latter will be supported by the
country; "it is the honour of the Church of England
that all her children and obedient people are full of
indignation against rebels, be they of any interest or
party whatsoever." But as he proceeds with his disquisition, events are running faster than his pen, and
he lifts his eyes from the page to see all Israel scattered
upon the mountains as sheep that have no shepherd.
Yet his spirits rise again; he thinks that the authority
and seemliness of Episcopacy have only to be made
manifest for those who have rebelled to lay down
their arms and crave for pardon. He sets himself to

prove, with a myriad of instances borrowed from "the holy primitives," that "the bishop is the bond and ligature of the Church's unity," and "separation from the bishop a symbol of faction." He arrogates "a capacity to the bishops" to undertake charges of public trust, — "it serves the King, it assists the Republic." He attacks with scorn "the white and watery colours of lay-elders." It is not probable that his arguments convinced a single Puritan in those angry days. His proofs of the necessity of absolute forms of Church government have not found favour with later theologians; even Bishop Heber, an enthusiast for the author, dismisses *Episcopacy Asserted* with the remark that the reasons on which Taylor rests his position are as unsound as the position itself is *prima facie* questionable.

The treatise, however, served its controversial purpose; it closes, in particular, with a freedom and energy of writing which were highly appreciated in the Oxford circle of Royalist scholars. On the 1st of November, by royal mandate, Taylor received the degree of doctor of divinity; and early in the following year he was presented to a sinecure which was still vaguely within the influence of the king, that of Overstone, between Northampton and Wellingborough. It is not improbable that this appointment was connected with his friendship with the Earl and Countess of Northampton, a relation which seems to have escaped the notice of all Jeremy Taylor's biographers. But Spencer Compton, second Earl of Northampton, was not only the friend of Taylor, but apparently his patron, and his remarkable influence on the literary work of the divine will be mentioned

later on. Of this Lord Northampton too little is
preserved; as Clarendon said, he was "not known
until his evening." After living a retired life in the
enjoyment of his great wealth, he suddenly developed
remarkable public energy at the breaking out of the
Civil War. Charles I. perceived his singular importance, and in November 1642, after the battle of Edgehill, Northampton was put in charge of the whole
district in Northamptonshire and Oxfordshire which
surrounded Banbury. He was extremely active, until
his brilliant career was cut short, at the age of forty-
two, at the battle of Hopton Heath, on the 19th of
March 1643. When we consider that Taylor was his
valued friend, and that Overstone was within what
we may call Lord Northampton's military district, it
is hard to believe that the appointment had no connection with the kindness either of the earl or of his
lady. The widowed Countess Mary — who was the
daughter of the poet of *Bosworth Field*, Sir John
Beaumont — remained the protector of Taylor, and
he described her afterwards, in reference to her kindness to him, as "hugely forward to entertain any
instrument whereby she might grow and increase in
the service of God and the charities of human people."
Nothing seems to me more likely than that, when
Taylor's wife and children were forced to leave
Uppingham, Lady Northampton found a temporary
asylum for them, half-way to Oxford, at Overstone.
Meanwhile it is to be observed that as Lord Northampton died early in 1643, and as he had been since
the breaking out of the war closely engaged in military
business, the long conversations in which "that excellent person" discussed theological literature with

Jeremy Taylor were probably held before the summer of 1642.[1]

The favour which Christopher Hatton enjoyed with the king was now steadily on the increase. Various distinctions were conferred upon him; he was raised to the peerage as Lord Hatton of Kirby in the summer of 1643, and before the winter of that year was out, was appointed Comptroller of the King's Household, a post which he held as long as Charles had a household to be comptrolled. Hatton's friendship for Taylor became still more practically intimate after this appointment, and, as chaplain-in-ordinary and general manager of household business, the two were brought into constant intercourse. A curious incident unites the names of these companions in a manner difficult to unravel. In 1644 a volume was published at Oxford, called *The Psalter of David*, " by the Right Honourable Christopher Hatton." A manuscript note by Anthony à Wood, in a copy of the first edition, however, informs us that it was really composed by Jeremy Taylor, and after the death of both, on the title-page of the eighth edition, the name of Taylor was quietly substituted for that of Hatton by the publisher of 1672. Roger North says that Lord Hatton " had bright parts, and

---

[1] The parochial registers of Overstone, unfortunately, begin with the year of Jeremy Taylor's death, 1667. The Earl of Winchilsea and Nottingham very kindly allowed me to search the vast accretions of his family papers for undescribed letters of Jeremy Taylor which were believed to exist there. These, unhappily, could not be discovered, but during the investigation we came by accident upon a deed of Charles I., with his great seal, granting the rectory of Overstone to Taylor. It is on this document, which remained in Lord Hatton's possession, that the statements in the text are founded.

professed also to be religious." Eden, although he
rejected the *Psalter* from Taylor's works, was inclined
to think that he had a hand in preparing it for the
press. It is a little edition of the Psalms, interspersed
with collects, and intended for "the closets of divers
devout persons." Nothing can be more natural than
that Hatton should propose and design such a work,
and should employ Taylor to carry it out under his
supervision.

For the next two years, to follow the fortunes of
Jeremy Taylor is to trace the adventures of the royal
household to which he was attached. Fuller had fled
to Oxford, but neither he nor Chillingworth was in
complete sympathy with the king or with his courtiers,
and both soon passed elsewhere, Chillingworth to die
of a wound received early in 1644 at the siege of
Arundel. With Fuller, his one great literary rival, it
does not seem that Taylor had any relations; they
appear to have lived side by side each unconscious of
the other. On the 6th of May 1644 *Mercurius Aulicus*
reports that the members have placed one Isaac Massey
to preach at Uppingham, in the place of the true
pastor, Doctor Jeremy Taylor, whose house had been
"plundered, his estate seized, and his family driven
out of doors." But the latter statement probably
refers to events of the previous year. On the 3rd of
June 1644, the exodus from Oxford began, and there
were weary months of marching and counter-marching
before, on the 23rd of November, the king re-entered
that city in triumph. That temporary exultation soon
sank in the depression of the poverty and distress at
Oxford, where early in 1645 a wretchedness approaching to famine dismayed the royalist garrison. On

January 10th, Taylor's earliest and most efficient friend, Laud, was executed. On the 7th of May the king marched out with his army towards the north, leaving Oxford to be starved up to the verge of submission. To and fro, through the Midland counties, Charles conducted his followers in vague and ineffectual man-oeuvres. By what means Jeremy Taylor became separated from the king's household it is impossible to determine; but he was with Colonel Charles Gerard when that general was defeated in trying to relieve Cardigan Castle on the 4th of February 1645, and he was among the prisoners captured by the Parlia-mentarians.

The campaign in South Wales raged up and down the valley of the Teify, and particularly round Cardigan Castle, which was the strategic base of that position. It was the brilliant Parliamentary general, Rowland Laugharne, who captured Cardigan at Christmas time 1644, although held by a strong garrison, who defended it " until a semi-culverine of brass, belonging to the *Leopard*, was mounted and played three days upon them, forcing a breach which was gallantly entered." On the 22nd of January 1645, Gerard, descending the Teify to check the invaders, was repulsed, and again, as we have seen, on the 4th of February, when Taylor must have been captured. Laugharne pushed on, impeded by his prisoners and his booty, to the investi-ture of Newcastle Emlyn, on the southern bank of the Teify, a strong fortress which was the key to Carmar-thenshire. Had the Parliamentarians stormed this place, they must have overrun the county. But on the 23rd of April the garrison of Newcastle Emlyn, taking advantage of their magnificent base, attacked

the army of Laugharne, and completely routed it.
Among the prisoners released by this turn in the
fortunes of war, Taylor may possibly have been included. But it is more likely that he had been left
behind in Cardigan Castle, and was now exchanged.
It is to be noted, perhaps, that he must originally
have started from Newcastle Emlyn with Gerard when
he marched to attack Laugharne, and that this fortress
(the New Castle of Emlyn) was the property and one
of the residences of that Earl of Carbery (whose
courtesy title was Lord Emlyn) who was shortly to be,
if he was not already, Taylor's next patron. We are
certain, however, only of the fact that he had now
fallen into the hands of the enemy.

Of the events which followed this catastrophe Taylor
gives the following account, in language that is tanta-
lisingly guarded : —

"In this great storm which hath dashed the vessel of the
Church all in pieces, I have been cast upon the coast of Wales,
and in a little boat thought to have enjoyed that rest and quietness which in England in a greater I could not hope for. Here
I cast anchor, and thinking to ride safely, the storm followed
me with so impetuous violence, that it broke a cable, and I lost
my anchor. And here again I was exposed to the mercy of the
sea, and the gentleness of an element that could neither distinguish things nor persons. And but that He, who stilleth the
raging of the sea, and the noise of His waves, and the madness
of His people, had provided a plank for me, I had been lost to
all the opportunities of content or study. But I know not
whether I have been more preserved by the courtesies of my
friends, or the gentleness and mercies of a noble enemy."

From the opening words of this passage we must
infer that when Taylor left the king, and retreated to

South Wales, it was with the idea of settling to clerical work, not, as has been supposed, of marching as a soldier, since the "little boat" is manifestly contrasted with the "greater" of Oxford. Then, after the capture at Cardigan, from which it is said that he was quickly released, we are here instructed that after being in imminent danger from the Puritan army which was sweeping South Wales, Jeremy Taylor was saved by the joint action of his friends and of "a noble enemy." The identity of the latter is unknown, and has greatly puzzled Taylor's annotators. Heber ingeniously argued that it must be Colonel Laugharne, his captor and the governor of Pembroke Castle, but of this there is no evidence whatever. Nor do I believe that, in the parlance of the seventeenth century, Laugharne or any other of the men who came to the front in Pembroke-shire as the leaders of the popular cause, would be styled a "noble" enemy. This points to one who was technically a nobleman, and unless we may conjecture that Essex was corresponded with, I confess that I am quite at a loss to identify Taylor's possible deliverer. It would greatly simplify our inquiry if we could per-suade ourselves that the "noble enemy" was Richard Vaughan, second Earl of Carbery, with whom Jeremy Taylor was now about to take up his abode at Golden Grove.

The difficulty is that Lord Carbery was, at least nominally, a royalist, and therefore no "enemy." But the passage which has just been quoted appeared in 1647, in the preface to *The Liberty of Prophesying*, a book primarily intended to be read by the king. Taylor's language is veiled in an allusive obscurity which is almost unintelligible unless we suppose that to

D

have been lucid would have been to be guilty of indis-
cretion. Now, it is certain that Taylor's position at
Golden Grove was rendered doubly delicate, and yet,
with care, doubly secure, by the ambiguous political
attitude of Lord Carbery. That nobleman belonged
to a type of moderates, few in number in that hour
and place, who sympathised with liberty of conscience,
while deploring the excesses of the fanatics, and who
wished to support the king, while detesting his
obstinacy and ignorance. He was, in fact, exactly
what, a little later and with great injustice, grew
to be called a "trimmer," and all we know of his
character fits in with Halifax's inimitable description
of the man who could "distinguish and desire a mean
between the sauciness of some of the Scotch apostles,
and the undecent courtship of some of the silken
divines, who do practise to bow at the altar only to
learn to make the better legs at court."

Lord Carbery, who was for many years to be the
protector and companion of Jeremy Taylor, was at
this time a man of between forty and fifty years of
age. His position as one of the wealthiest landlords
in South Wales gave him great local importance, and
when the Civil War broke out, his loyalty to the
king was unquestioned. He organised the formation
of militia in his own counties of Carmarthen and
Cardigan, and after the first battles he was appointed
lieutenant-governor of the army in these shires, and
in that of Pembroke. But he showed little zeal, and
less as time went on. Doubtless he grew increasingly
disturbed by doubts of the entire justice of the royalist cause. Meanwhile, there were opposed to him the
energy and rapidity of Rowland Laugharne; and

Lord Carbery became more and more languid as a general. In March 1644 his troops were driven out of Pembrokeshire, and he took the opportunity to resign his appointment in favour of Gerard. He withdrew to his house of Golden Grove, and rumours were soon current of his cultivating the company of his opponents too tamely, until it was more than hinted that his allegiance was dubious. He was certainly the friend and correspondent of Essex; he was no less certainly treated with singular mildness by the victorious Parliamentarians. Later on in the story we shall find him acquiescing contentedly in the action of the House of Commons. The loyalists broadly impeached both his integrity and his courage. But there is no evidence that Lord Carbery was a coward; he was a "trimmer" in the original sense. He was a tolerant and thoughtful man, whose conscience hung in the balance between two causes, and gradually leaned over on the liberal side. But by 1647, when Jeremy Taylor wrote his dedication, Carbery might well be regarded by Charles I. as a "noble enemy."

The storm of 1645, however, cast Taylor, deprived of books, effects, and means, into "a private corner of the world," as Rust tells us, where "a tender providence shrouded him under her wings, and the prophet was fed in the wilderness." In a romantic valley of Carmarthenshire, an Oxford friend of Taylor's, William Wyatt, had recently joined the distinguished grammarian, Dr. William Nicholson, to help him in starting a private school. Taylor may well have known Nicholson also, since the future Bishop of Gloucester was a frequent visitor to Oxford. Since 1626, Nicholson had been rector of Llandilo-

vawr, and Wyatt of Llanfihangel-Aberbythych, the
church of which was contiguous, on the west side,
with the park of Golden Grove. In the rectory, we
may suppose, the storm-tossed fugitive was originally
received, while suggestions were being made for
"supplying him with bread and necessaries." One
of the earliest initiations would naturally be to take
him to the great house, where the general patron,
Lord Carbery, fell under Taylor's customary spell,
welcomed him to Golden Grove, and presently made
him his chaplain.

These household duties did not prevent him from
joining Nicholson and Wyatt in their school, which
was held at a house called Newton Hall, which
Nicholson rented. This "private academy" was
highly successful, until the Restoration rendered its
revenue needless to its principal founders. Wood
says that "several youths were most loyally edu-
cated there, and afterwards sent to the universities."
Of these, young Christopher Hatton, the future first
Viscount Hatton, was one, and another was the
boy who afterwards became a judge, Sir John
Powell, and who in 1650 was matriculated from
Newton Hall, or Collegium Newtoniense, as the fond
pedantry of its founders preferred to call it. Other
obscurer pupils have recorded their appreciation of
their masters, who, in 1647, issued a *Grammar*,
apparently a joint production, to which Jeremy
Taylor contributed a florid dedication in English.

A third means of support remained within Taylor's
reach, his pen. But on his first arrival at Llanfihangel-Aberbythych he was sadly hampered by the want
of books. He had been accustomed, in his Oxford

days, to that excessive and almost incessant reference
to authorities, which was so devastating to the prose
of that age, and particularly to its theology. In his
present retirement he felt, at first, helpless away from
a library; in the "voisinage" of Golden Grove there
were no volumes of a casuistical species, and it was
long before he took courage to make bricks without
patristic straw. He waited to begin to write in Wales,
he tells us, until he felt that he "needed no other
books or aids than what a man carries with him on
horseback." Then he became, for the first time, a free
writer and a great master of English. But, at the
beginning, his spirits were too far cast down, and his
hopes too shattered to enable him to do more than his
ordinary daily business. He suffered, after the shock
of his disaster and his peril, from a severe reaction,
during which he could do no more than brood over
"the public dyscrasy" — as he loves to call it —
and all the calamities of his Church and country.
"I had seen my design blasted in the bud," he
says, "and I despaired in the Calends of doing what
I purposed in the Ides before." But gradually this
melancholy passed away, and he turned to literary
labour.

He now secured the valuable co-operation of the
eminent royalist publisher, Richard Royston, who, in
1647, bought up the remainders of Taylor's early works,
and issued them with his own imprint. Royston, who
was to be Taylor's publisher for the future, was a man of
much capacity and resource. He was the leader of his
profession all through the middle of the seventeenth
century, and when he died, full of wealth and consideration, in 1686, he was nearly ninety years of age.

Royston was "bookseller to three kings," and in his loyalist enthusiasm frequently got into trouble during the Commonwealth. He was accused, and with perfect justice, of being " a constant factor for all scandalous books " against the decrees of the House of Commons. His relations with Jeremy Taylor, although strained once or twice, were on the whole creditable and advantageous to both.

In the remainder of this chapter we will confine ourselves to a rapid survey of Jeremy Taylor's publications during the first four years of his residence at Golden Grove, because they all belong, in conception if not in execution, to the earlier period of his career. Although he was stripped, after Cardigan, of all his papers, so that he became " full of apprehension that I should live unprofitably, and die obscurely, and be forgotten," it is evident that he must have left some of his manuscripts at All Souls, whence they were afterwards partly sent to him. This is confirmed by the fact that at least one manuscript, that of his *Reverence due to the Altar*, being mislaid, remained at Oxford. The first work which Taylor prepared at Golden Grove for the press was that which is now generally known as *An Apology for Liturgy*, part of which appeared anonymously, as *A Discourse concerning Prayer*, towards the close of 1646. Taylor found means to bring this surreptitious issue under the notice of Charles I.; and he produced the complete work, with a daring dedication, " to his most sacred majesty," just before the king's execution; this should not be overlooked as a proof of Taylor's fidelity and courage.

An Apology for Liturgy was a very popular work among the High Church party, and was often reprinted

in the course of Taylor's life. It is a reply to the
decisions of the House of Commons as embodied in
the ordinance of January 1645, by which the Book of
Common Prayer was abolished, and a Directory of
Worship set up to enforce uniformity. But it is not
necessary to suppose that Taylor waited for this enact-
ment, which was but the official promulgation of views
which had been loudly expressed for three years past.
The beauty and fitness for its purpose of the English
liturgy in its entire constitution, the "ghostly advantage" of employing it, the quality of the priest's power
in absolution, the importance of praying to God "with
consideration," the scandal of allowing the ecclesiastical
regiment to become a democracy, all these were themes
familiar to his thoughts, although the action of the
Directory compelled him to publication.

From a literary point of view, *An Apology for Liturgy*
shows a growing freedom in style. The colloquial turn
of some of the sentences, and the use of "Well!" in
argument, betray the orator beneath the casuist. The
treatise is rather rich in faint autobiographical touches.
Taylor's romantic attachment to the set forms of
worship takes beautiful shapes: "I can but with joy
and eucharist consider with what advantages and
blessings the pious protestant is entertained, and
blessed, and armed against all his needs, by the constant and religious usage of the Common Prayer
Book." We listen with pleasure while he dilates on
his own singular relish in the collects, and his joy in
the forms of confession and praise. His idea of prayer
was of something deliberate and stately; he did not
believe in impromptu devotion, or worship conducted
without art or deliberation. He faintly and grudgingly

admits the use of private extempore prayer, but
evidently disparages it, and asks why the Holy
Spirit should fly from us at the sight of an ink-horn.
Jeremy Taylor himself wrote down all his prayers.
In *An Apology for Liturgy* we find him still intolerant,
still the enemy of every sort of innovation. The
change, therefore, to his next public appearance is
something startling.

On the 28th of June 1647 was published a work,
the importance of which cast all Taylor's previous
productions into insignificance. *The Liberty of Pro-*
phesying was his first long book, and it was his first
independent book. In it, for the first time, he came
forward as a great theological innovator. It is true, as
S. R. Gardiner has pointed out, that "three-fourths of its
argument were written under the influence of Chillingworth's " *Religion of a Protestant*. Doubtless all those
walks in Oxford gardens, at the close of which Chillingworth had found cause gently to complain of Taylor's
inattention, had produced far more effect on the
younger divine than the elder supposed. Nevertheless, the attitude of Taylor in 1647 was a profoundly individual one, and in one respect, and that
the most important, it owed nothing to a predecessor.
Chillingworth's entire interest had been swallowed up
in his analysis of English divergencies from Rome.
In the general "dyscrasy" Taylor gave little thought
to the Papal system; he was absorbed in the troubles
nearer home. He has still to be fighting along the
narrow Anglican ridge, but his sword is turned mainly
now towards the side of Geneva.

The sword, however, though still unsheathed, takes
a far less prominent place than the palm-branch in *The*

Liberty of Prophesying. The discourse opens with a yearning cry for amity. The Oxford attitude, the old Laudian arrogance, have given way to a softer tolerance. Jeremy Taylor has grown gentle and meek in his adversity. He is no longer "hasty in calling every disliked opinion by the name of heresy." There is, we must perhaps admit, the natural difference which comes over the advocate of a majority when he has to appeal for a minority. The natural timidity of Taylor, the too easily fluttered spirits, have to be taken into account. As Canon Hensley Henson has put it, "his sense of the inherent wrongfulness of forcing conscience was quickened by the discomforts of his lot." But these do not explain the sudden burst of intellectual and moral liberality which make *The Liberty of Prophesying* such a stimulating volume. We read it with enthusiasm, because it shows a real and surprising growth in virtue and wisdom.

The spirit which inspires the author of this treatise is the hope to see the English Church, over which the flood has swept, repair its scattered ruins, and be redintegrated in a new Pentecost. He sees that this may be done by the way of peace. He has the brilliant intuition that if the divided tongues of the Spirit are of the same fire, their different operation may be left to lead automatically towards a more splendid illumination of truth. From this conception of unity in difference, casting out the ugliness of discord, *The Liberty of Prophesying* starts, and the author develops, on these lines, a courageous, and, in spite of what had been said by earlier and more partial opponents of tyranny, in the main a perfectly novel plea for the right of religious liberty. The book is inspired by

the warmest and the most delicate Christian charity,
expounded at an hour and in a country where passion
had made charity almost appear untenable. It had
occurred to Taylor in his solitude that the general
violence of religious anger in England was as absurd
as it was hateful; that it must be "inconsistent with
God's goodness to condemn those who err when the
error hath nothing of the will in it." Every man
must be left free to find out, according to his best
lights, what is truth to him. It is the sin against the
heavenly vision which is the worst offence, and after
all "no man's spirit is known to any but to God and
himself." On the other hand, as has been pointed out,
Taylor had the signal independence to oppose the
theory which was almost universal in the Puritan
society of his day, and which was eminently defended
by Milton, that sectarianism itself was praiseworthy.

The importance of this wonderful book, from the
theological and philosophical side, is so great that
many writers have not scrupled to give it the highest
place among the works of its author. Without under-
valuing it in the least, however, it must be pointed out
that on purely literary grounds *The Liberty of Prophesying* can lay no claim to such pre-eminence. It is
written in a style very clear, simple, and unadorned,
with a sweetness of temper entirely characteristic of
its writer, and with none or few of those impediments,
those pedantic snags in the current, which had hitherto
impeded the course of Taylor's language. He bitterly
deplores his separation from his books; but we may
rejoice at his release from their bondage. He still has
his beloved *Prudentius,* and his not less valued *Horace,*
and he is more free to use them, now that his shelves

are no longer crowded with folio Fathers. He does not regret his past study of the schoolmen, but has abandoned them for the present; he recognises their weak logic and their contradictions and their narrowness; he laughs out loud at the folly of Pope Adrian VI. in believing that "all poetry was heretical." But with all the amenity and all the eloquence of *The Liberty of Prophesying*, it does not exhibit to us the glory of Taylor. It is bare and a little dry in statement; there is a remarkable absence of that pomp of imagery which is characteristic of his finest writing. Its lucidity is slightly humdrum; it presents few passages which could be separated from their context, and exhibited as specimens of English. But that his style, though still unadorned, had become admirably pure and direct, a fragment of narrative, not untouched with humour, may exemplify : —

"It was an argument of some wit, but of singularity of understanding, that happened in the great contestation between the missals of S. Ambrose and S. Gregory. The lot was thrown, and God made to be judge, so as He was tempted to a miracle to answer a question which themselves might have ended without much trouble. The two missals were laid upon the altar, and the church door shut and sealed. By the morrow matins they found S. Gregory's missal torn in pieces and thrown about the church, but S. Ambrose's opened and laid upon the altar in a posture of being read. If I had been to judge of the meaning of this miracle, I should have made no scruple to have said it had been the will of God that the missal of S. Ambrose, which had been anciently used and publicly tried and approved of, should still be read in the Church. And that of Gregory let alone, it being torn by an angelical hand as an argument of its imperfection, or of the inconvenience of innovation. But yet they judged it otherwise. For, by the tearing and scattering about, they thought

it was meant it should be used over all the world, and that
of S. Ambrose read only in the church of Milan. I am more
satisfied that the former was the true meaning than I am of
the truth of the story ; but we must suppose that."

The attitude of Taylor must not be confounded with
that which had been adopted as early as 1641 by
Williams, and after the battle of Edgehill by the
party of Holles. Fuller had reminded the House of
Commons, unwilling listeners to his plea, that "Blessed
are the peace-makers," and others less eloquent than
he had desired to discover for the Church of England
a middle path between Laud and the Presbyterians.
There had been a desire expressed, here and there, in
intervals of weariness after the clash of arms, for rest
in a reasonable common creed. The Puritans were to
concede some points on their side, the Episcopalians
to push their demands less stringently ; extremists
were to avoid running a-tilt against the scruples of
their neighbours. Fuller, for instance, while he was
hopeful that the king would show " a fair condescen-
sion in matters of church reformation," denied "any
transcendent extraordinary miraculous light" to the
lay preachers of the Separatists. Williams was more
outspoken in his famous pamphlet, *The Bloody Tenet
of Persecution* (1644), in which he deprecated all re-
course to the civil arm, and recommended for the cor-
rection of spiritual offences a spiritual censure. As
Gardiner has excellently said, all these preluders of
the principle of toleration longed for peace through
mutual concession. As much may be said for the
anonymous author of that very remarkable tract,
Liberty of Conscience, of which the same historian
has given so valuable an account ; although that

also marks a stage along the road of humanity and charity.

In spite of the liberality shown, on certain points, by Cromwell, in spite of Milton's voice lifted so nobly in *Comus* and *Areopagitica*, in spite, too, of the glimmerings exhibited by that odd group of dissenters who were called the Independents, it cannot be said that liberty of conscience, in the broad and modern sense, was brought before the minds of Englishmen until Jeremy Taylor published his *Liberty of Prophesying*. It is an extraordinary proof of the vigour of his mind, that he, of all men living, trained at Cambridge and Oxford in the very mysteries of Thorough, the *protégé* of Laud, the companion of Juxon and Sheldon, should, without passing through any violent crisis, by the sheer evolution of his piety and tenderness, have broken through the thickest crust of prejudice. This danger of being misunderstood or too well understood was extreme; and if his situation had not been eminently propitious, it is probable that he could not have dared to affront the fanaticism of the age with paragraphs so outspoken as the following: —

"Well, thus far are we come! Although we are secured in fundamental points from involuntary error by the plain express, and dogmatical places of Scripture, yet in other things we are not, and may be invincibly mistaken, because of the obscurity and difficulty in the controverted parts of Scripture. . . . Councils are contradictory to each other, and therefore certainly are equally deceived, many of them. Then the Popes of Rome are very likely to mislead us, but cannot ascertain us of truth in matter of question. And in this world we believe in part, and prophesy in part, and this imperfection shall never be done away till we be transplanted to a more glorious state. Either, then, we must throw our chances and

get truth by accident or predestination, or else we must lie safe
in a mutual toleration and private liberty of persuasion, unless
some other anchor can be thought upon where we may fasten
our floating vessels and ride safely."

Here we have the note which was so absolutely
novel in Taylor. Those who preceded him by a year
or two, in their meditations on a possible religious
peace, had conceived a plan of mutual concession, of
agreement upon common essentials. But it was Taylor who first conceived of a toleration not founded
upon agreement or concession, but upon a broad
basis of practical piety, of loyal confidence in that
church which, as he says in one of his luminous
phrases, "is not a chimera, or a shadow, but a company of men believing in Jesus Christ," and therefore
able to trust the *bona fides* of others who approach the
same truth from a different standpoint. He called
the sour fanatics of his time — and in 1644 not to be a
fanatic of some sort was almost to be a changeling or
pariah — back to the humane and merciful doctrine
of Jesus Christ, "whose lessons were softer than nard
or the juice of the Candian olive." In an age altogether given up to proscription and persecution,
Jeremy Taylor lifted his clear voice in proof of "the
unreasonableness of prescribing to other men's faith,
and the iniquity of persecuting differing opinions."

It is not too much to claim for Taylor, in the religious and intellectual order, something of the gratitude which we all pay, or should by common justice
pay, to Sir James Simpson in the physical order. It
would be impossible to estimate the alleviation which
Taylor's tolerant theory, in its successive extensions,
has brought to the multitudes of men. Such horrors

in the cruel chastisement of impiety as followed the
battle of Naseby were to be impossible again among
civilised Englishmen as long as the world should last.
It was gradually to be understood that sin is not to
be punished by torture, and that the liberal opinion
that "all papists, and anabaptists, and sacramentaries,
are fools and wicked persons" was no longer to be an
excuse for ferocious reprisals. Those, and all errors
which are of the head and not the heart, were to be
treated for the future with argument and a meek
humility, — the blessed anæsthetics which this great
innovator introduced into the practice of religious
surgery. What the world has gained in loss of pain
is incalculable. There is, perhaps, no man to-day in
England, who worships, or who worships not, as his
conscience bids him, who does not owe a fraction of
his peace to Jeremy Taylor.

Even in the shades of Golden Grove, and close to
the rural "Church of the Angels," such a novel doctrine could not be promulgated without danger. Of
course Taylor was careful to guard himself from mis-
conception; equally, of course, he was instantly mis-
conceived. He was careful to limit his plea for
toleration to those who unite in the Christian Creed,
but this was of slight importance in that day, when, in
the civilised parts of Europe, it would have been difficult to discover persons not Jews or atheists not nominally covered by this general confession. He does not
say, so far as I have been able to discover, a single
word which would exclude from toleration those outside the Christian pale; he merely does not consider
them. He seems to admit that if there come into
being religious systems which teach rebellion or im-

morality, these may be subdued by force of arms. This was, perhaps, illogical, but some such admission was inevitable in the face of the war at that moment raging in these islands, a war which Taylor's loyalty to the king would not permit him to stigmatise directly. In every legitimate mode, with every phrase of moderation, he sought to conciliate those whom his theory of toleration might be expected to wound and startle.

Of these, the first was the king himself. When *The Liberty of Prophesying* was published, Charles I. had recently been seized, after that vivid scene in the garden at Holmby, and had been carried about the country, an embarrassing hostage, by Joyce and his troops. This had been the opening of the fifth act of his tragedy, and now Charles was in more need than any of his subjects of the nard and balsam of charity. By the time Taylor's book could reach him, he was ensconced at Caversham under Lord Craven's care, and there he read, no doubt with fervent interest, the new book of his old chaplain. Intolerant as were his enemies, however, they met with a narrowness no less stubborn in the king. Even in his hour of humiliation — "causeless they like a bird have chasèd me" — Charles I. could not accept the principle of a free conscience. He expressed his displeasure to his chaplains, and he instructed one of them, Dr. Henry Hammond, who was an old personal friend of Taylor, and had succeeded him in the royal household, to frame a reply.

The gentle and dignified Hammond was one of the most uplifted spirits who were gathered about Charles I. in his decline; he had been made his private chaplain in Oxford in 1644, and he kept near him in spite of all

machinations of the enemy, who specially dreaded his
influence, until Christmas of this year, 1647, when the
king was deprived of all his servants.   Hammond was
famous for his lavish benevolence.   Although a great
deal of money passed into his hands, he was always
poor, for he was always giving.   He had much in
common with Taylor; like him, Hammond had written in defence of Episcopacy and of the liturgy; and
later on in this very year he published *The Christian's
Obligation to Peace and Charity*.   In this, however, his
views are conventional, and show no grasp of Jeremy
Taylor's position.   It was in his *Letter of Resolution*
that Hammond embodied what seem to have been the
king's main objections to *Liberty of Prophesying*, in a
discussion of "six Quarés."   He traverses Taylor's
already surprising views about the baptism of children
and rebukes his mildness to Anabaptists.   But there
is no venom in Hammond.   He praises the "diligence" of the very arguments he refutes, and is
everywhere inspired by friendliness and courtesy.

There were many attacks of a severer kind made
against Taylor's volume.   According to Heber, who
undertook an examination of these pamphlets, most of
which are obscure and insignificant, the most serious
was that made by Samuel Rutherford of St. Andrews, in
his *Free Disputation against pretended Liberty of Conscience*.   Nor would this savage libel deserve the briefest
mention here, were it not that its sordid existence curiously links with the name of Jeremy Taylor those of
Milton and of S. T. Coleridge.   It is supposed that
Milton, who already admired Taylor's genius, and had
read *The Liberty of Prophesying* with approval, was so
much incensed at Rutherford's odious defence of per-

E

secution and his attack on the gentle charity of Taylor,
that, in his sonnet on the "New Forces," he expressed
his horror that a "Scotch what d'ye call" should venture to speak in such terms of opprobrium as Rutherford used for Taylor; and that

> "Men whose life, learning, faith and pure intent
>   Would have been held in high esteem with Paul,
>   Must now be nam'd and printed heretics."

This conjunction of Milton and Jeremy Taylor, in its
turn, called forth a century and a half later, from the
youthful S. T. Coleridge, an encomiastic parallel of the
genius of these two men, which is one of the most
splendid tributes to Taylor ever written.

A little later in the summer of 1647, we have a
glimpse of Charles I. at Caversham, reported by Sir
Philip Warwick, who was permitted a very brief interview with him : —

"I could perceive" (writes Warwick) "he was very apprehensive in what hands he was, but was not to let it be discerned. Nor had he given his countenance unto Dr. Taylor's
Liberty of Prophesying, which some believed he had ; but that
really and truly it was refreshment to his spirit to be used with
some civility, and to serve God as he was wont, and to see some
old faces about him."

The wording of this phrase seems to convey that
Charles had been reproached by his Puritan jailers
with his supposed approval of his former chaplain's
revolutionary sentiments, with regard to liberty of
conscience, and that he was anxious to remove this
impression. Probably very few persons, in either
camp, were content at first to accept Taylor's position,
but he had sown good seed. Meanwhile, in August

Charles was brought up to Putney, whence in November
he fled to the Isle of Wight, still ready in his amazing
blindness to be *Pater Patriæ* on his own terms.   But
he was approaching the end of his career, and from
Christmas 1647, he was a helpless prisoner in Caris-
brooke Castle.

The year 1648 was one of extreme disturbance in
South Wales, and must have included the most anxious
months of Taylor's residence there.   Laugharne, his
old enemy, veered round to the king's side, and an
officer of his, Poyer, taking the initiative, drove the
Parliamentarians out of Pembrokeshire in March.
South Wales suddenly declared for the king.   Horton
was sent down to meet the mutineers, and in April
Poyer marched his army across Carmarthenshire to
check him, passing close to Golden Grove.   By the
end of the month, the whole of the neighbourhood was
in revolt, and as Horton advanced the Welsh fled to
their hills.   The business was so serious that Cromwell
himself was sent down from London, but before he
reached South Wales, Horton had routed Laugharne
and the rebels at the battle of St. Fagans, near Llandaff,
on the 8th of May.   The revolt was crushed, but
Cromwell's advance brought terror before it.   He captured Chepstow Castle on the 25th, and then marched
westwards through Glamorganshire and Carmarthenshire.   His direct road brought him across the Towey
at the town of Llandilovawr, where he was almost in
sight of Golden Grove: he must have reached this
point on or about the 28th of May, 1648.

Cromwell's approach threw Lord Carbery into a
violent apprehension.   The general was presently seen,
with a troop of horse, riding across country towards

Golden Grove. The pacific owner of that estate, who
had already, we are told, been "pardoned" by Laugharne, was now in danger of seeing all his property
sequestered by Laugharne's conqueror. On receiving
news that Cromwell was coming, the earl fled across
the fields to one of his remoter farms, leaving his
countess to receive their alarming guest. Lady Carbery, no doubt, was encouraged to believe that she
could plead her husband's cause with success, if only,
like Lady Verney two years earlier, she could "bring
her spirit to a soliciting temper, and tell how to use
the juice of an onion to soften" her visitor's heart. It
was in this spirit that the countess received Cromwell
at the doors of Golden Grove, and civilly invited him
to dismount. The resident chaplain would, as a
matter of course, be at her side to support her; and we
cannot doubt that Taylor's exquisite amenity and
courtesy had their share in bringing about the surprising result. Cromwell, who came to sequester,
stayed to dine; and in the afternoon pursued his
march to the beleaguerment of Tenby and Pembroke.
The antiquary, who tells the anecdote, does not in so
many words inform us what concessions were made at
the dinner-table. But Lord Carbery, of all the magnates
of South Wales, alone escaped sequestration. With
what a sigh of relief the crafty lady and her chaplain
must have seen the horsemen move away towards
Carmarthen, and with what haste a messenger must
have been sent to fetch the earl home from his hiding-
place ! Lord Carbery, who was the most conspicuous
trimmer of the province, gave no further cause of suspicion to Parliament, and was left undisturbed. It
would even seem that Oliver Cromwell recalled his

visit to Lady Carbery with pleasure, for a few years later he sent down several stags to furnish the park at Golden Grove.

The king's fortunes were the subject of anxious solicitude to Jeremy Taylor, and he discussed them with zest and prolixity. In this same year, 1648, he had a meeting with Dr. Thomas Bayly, who had been closely identified with Charles I. at Raglan Castle. Bayly professed to guide the king's conscience, and had published an imaginary conversation between the king and the Marquis of Worcester, which was much talked about at the moment. "What I delivered *in transitu*, when I had the happiness last to meet you, I know I poured into a breast locked up as religiously as the priests of Cybele," is a phrase which Taylor uses in a very long letter, addressed to Bayly on the Vigils of Christmas, 1648. According to his biographers, Bayly left England for France and Flanders in the latter part of 1646, and did not return until after the king's death, but this must be a mistake. Bayly was hardly worthy of Taylor's sympathy; he was a fussy and braggart Royalist who ultimately turned Romanist, attacked the institutions of England, and died obscurely in Italy.

Great, however, as was Jeremy Taylor's interest in passing events, and in the fate of those friends who were most dear to him, they did not occupy all his thoughts during these distracted years. In 1649 he completed, and gave to the world, a work of large proportions, and eminently original plan, which exhibited his literary powers as they had never been exhibited before. *The Great Exemplar* was in the purely intellectual field as novel an enterprise as *Liberty of*

Prophesying had been in the moral and controversial.
It was an attempt, on a huge scale, at the production
of a class of book, no specimen of which had been presented to the English public before, but which has been
abundantly imitated since, and has had its lasting influence on our literature. Before we consider the
peculiarly novel characteristics of this work, and its
disposition and structure, it will be well to bring together what can be recovered as to its history.

That it was not designed at Golden Grove, or even
mainly written there, is evident, from the part in its
preparation which was taken by Lord Northampton.
That nobleman, as we have seen, was killed at the
battle of Hopton Heath, early in 1643. His share,
therefore, in the conception of *The Great Exemplar* must
be precedent to that date ; and as he was closely engaged
in military duties from the breaking out of the Civil
War until his death, Taylor's communications with
him on the subject are probably not to be placed later
than the middle of 1642. But up to that time, if we
possessed no other evidence than that which has been
known to Taylor's biographers, we should be justified
in believing the divine to be a docile and unquestioning
disciple of the Oxford casuists, a submissive pupil of
Laud in the propaganda of Thorough, placed at All
Souls College, and remaining there, for the sole purpose of ministering to the cause by his patriotic learning and storehouse of instances.

It is, therefore, of extraordinary interest to learn
that at a date which cannot be later than 1642 a
single far-sighted friend had perceived that Taylor was
throwing away his genius upon "the spinosities of the
schools," and had determined to divert him into a

more primrose path. The language Jeremy Taylor
uses must be carefully examined. He says that the
Earl of Northampton's mind was the " soil " in which
" the first design of these papers," that is to say, of
The Great Exemplar, " grew "; that " what that rare
person conceived, I was left to the pains and danger
of bringing forth." The image here is exactly the same
which has fascinated and baffled successive generations
of Shakespearian critics. As W. H. was " the sole
begetter " of the *Sonnets*, so Lord Northampton was
the sole " conceiver " of *The Great Exemplar*. In each
case, it is not rational to doubt, there is an intention
to attribute to a noble friend the suggestion, the bias,
which led the writer along a new experiment in his
art. In each case, below the form of compliment, is a
statement of cause and effect which it is preposterous
to overlook or to minimise.

In Taylor's case, when he made his statement, the
widowed Countess of Northampton, who remained his
friend, was alive and well aware of the circumstances.
He appeals to her recollections: " Your Honour best
knows " how mere a matter of honesty it is for the
author to recall the facts. When the lady reads
the pages of *The Great Exemplar* she will recollect at
once that her late husband, " that excellent personage,
was their first root," and that they are " the fruits of
his," Lord Northampton's, " abode." This is a curious
phrase, but I take it to mean no more than his abode
on earth, before he was " transplanted to heaven " by
his sudden death. Lady Northampton is conjured to
welcome the book " for its first relation," that is to say,
no doubt, for the fact that its origin and substance will
both of them recall sad and yet proud memories to her

mind; and to set its imperfections down not to its
"fountain," her husband, but to Jeremy Taylor, who
is "the channel of its progress and emanation."

If these phrases have any meaning at all, it is plain
that they indicate that Lord Northampton, who must
have had close opportunities of studying the mind of
Taylor, was sorry to see so splendid a gift of rhetoric
and pathos expended on "problems and inactive discourses," that is to say on hair-splitting casuistry. He
persuaded the pupil of Laud and Richard Montagu
that it was "the nature of disputings, that they begin
commonly in mistakes, proceed with zeal and fancy, and
end not at all but in schisms and uncharitable names,
and too often dip their feet in blood." In saying this,
Lord Northampton found an eager listener. Humble
and tractable as Taylor was, and honest in his service
for Laud, he had to confess that he was "weary and
toiled with rowing up and down in the seas of questions which the interests of Christendom have com-
menced." The design which his noble friend sketched
out, and which the earl's premature death forbade him
to enjoy in its execution, was no less than this, "to put
a portion of the holy fire into a repository, which might
help to re-enkindle the incense, when it shall please
God religion shall return, and all His servants sing *In
convertendo captivitatem Sion* with a voice of eucharist."

If we turn to *The Great Exemplar* to see how this
experiment was carried out, we are first of all impressed
by the negative qualities of the book. It has none of
the dryness, none of the nakedness which had indis-
putably been the growing faults of English theology.
The author glances at the works of his contemporaries,
and he decides that "they may be learned, but they

are not wise." He will sacrifice the display of learning; there shall be no discussion of knotty points; he
will not write a thesis, or engage in a controversy, or
quote the opinions of contending fathers in a dry light
of "unprofitable and ineffective contemplation"; he
will make a living book, and address it to those "who
can believe and love," not to those that can merely
"consider and love." He has the boldest views about
his literary mission. He will not scold or argue,
he will entertain. He is afraid neither of the word nor
the idea; let us be equally bold, and admit that his
design is to please, even to enthrall. He rates the
theologians with their narrow range of intellectual
interest. He says that it is far wiser to read Homer,
Æschylus, and Euripides than to bury one's self in the
patristic triflings of the schoolmen.

He was not ignorant of the scandal which his book
would cause. It was not thought more decent for a
churchman to appear without his Latinity upon him
than to go up into the pulpit in secular habit. Even
Chillingworth had been blamed for pursuing his
theme on lines too logical, without the constant application of tags from the Church authorities; he had
been roundly accused of want of "learning." It required immense courage on Taylor's part to defy all the
criticism of his class, and fold away his unquestioned
erudition as a robe not fit to be worn on this particular
occasion. He says, "I have despised my own reputation"; he has written a popular book, "embossed with
unnecessary but graceful ornament." He knows that
his clerical brethren will be scandalised, but he believes
that he is divinely led. "My spark," he cries, "may
grow greater by kindling my brother's taper, and God

may be glorified in us both." So he bravely puts forth
the earliest modern treatise of popular piety, "inter-
mixing something of pleasure with the use," and not
shrinking from the hope that his readers will find in
it that "which will better entertain their spirits than
a romance." The result was a noble and too often
forgotten manual which was the pioneer of a whole
literature of piety.

The Great Exemplar is a celebration of the beauty of
the Lord Jesus, God and Man. The up-raised, ecstatic
movement of the paragraphs betrays the enthusiasm of
the writer; he is Christ-possessed. The most gracious
voice then to be heard in England is lifted like that of
a nightingale above the frogs and ravens of the age.
The form he adopts is interesting; it is cunningly
devised to sustain and divert the attention, to prevent
weariness, to prolong the pleasure of the reader by
division and variety. It opens with a preface, one of
Taylor's exquisitely winning introductions, in which
the great family of Man is described, the necessity
of discipline in its organism demonstrated, and Christianity shown to be the most perfect law conceivable
for its direction. Then, after an exhortation to the
imitation of Jesus, the romance begins.

The string on which the whole sequence of pearls
is hung is the narrative of the life of Christ on earth.
The author tells the story as he chooses. There is no
attempt at Biblical criticism, even as in those days
it was understood; no dealing with difficulties of
parallel Evangelists; no weighing of evidence. Taylor
selects such versions of the narrative as best suit his
purpose, not shrinking from the traditions of a later
age, if they attract him. For instance, he accepts

without a question the legend of the prostration of
the Egyptian gods when the Infant crossed the border.
If an incident inflames his imagination, he lingers over
it as long as he chooses; he weaves his fancy, for
instance, for page after page, around the apparition
of the Star of Epiphany. What he dwells upon, exclusively, is the imaginative and the pathetic. He
wishes to draw men away from the weariness of controversy to the exquisite mysteries of pure religion.

But he knows that sustained rhetoric fatigues the
mind. He is careful to vary his theme. Accordingly,
after each section of his narrative, he applies that fragment of the story to a disquisition on its practical
bearing upon life, to general remarks about men's
religious duty as illustrated by what he has just
described. He rivets the attention of his readers by
abrupt application of the history to the needs of
modern society, to the family, to the state, to friendship and to the conduct of affairs. Nor is this enough
to secure the cunning variety of his design, which is
further gained by the introduction of short prayers,
each like a gush of music. In these devotions, the
most exquisite of their kind in the English language,
Jeremy Taylor has had no rival. They display, in the
most complete manner, the delicate wholesomeness of
his conscience and the inimitable distinction of his
style. Nowhere does he open a well of English more
undefiled than in his admirable private prayers.

It has been made a matter for regret that all the
early sermons of Jeremy Taylor (for the lecture on
Gunpowder Plot was no true sermon) are lost to us.
The regret is needless; they are certainly embedded
in *The Great Exemplar*. The careful reader will

distinguish twenty "discourses" in the body of that work, and we may be sure that each of these was preached from a pulpit. It is obvious that it was the consideration of the rare originality and beauty of some of these sermons which inspired Lord Northampton with his fortunate idea of urging Jeremy Taylor to weave around them a popular life of Christ. Internal evidence would alone be sufficient to persuade us of this fact, were there not a point of external evidence which confirms it. Some years after Taylor's death, two manuscript sermons of his were discovered, and published in 1675: these are known as *Christ's Yoke an Easy Yoke* and *The Gate to Heaven a strait Gate*. They were issued together, with a new portrait of the bishop, and as having been supplied by "a person of honour yet living," probably the third Earl of Northampton, who did not die until 1681. Of these sermons, on examination, the first in its entirety, and portions of the second, are found in the mass of *The Great Exemplar*. They were inadvertently printed, as novelties, and no doubt from copies left behind him by Taylor in his flight to Wales in 1644.

It would be idle to pretend that there are not flaws in the execution of this wonderful book. It is not sustained throughout at the very high level of its finest sections. At its best, it is written with enchanting fluidity and sweetness, the bright, elastic phrase leaping into light. But we begin already to perceive that Jeremy Taylor has two manners, the one far less attractive than the other. When he says : —

"Filling the rooms of the understanding with airy and ineffective notions is just such an excellency as it is in a man

to imitate the voice of birds; at his very best the nightingale
shall excel him ";

or,

> "God's authority is like sacred fire in an earthen censer, as
> holy as if it were kindled with the fanning of a cherub's wing,
> or placed just under the propitiatory [1] upon a golden altar,"

the effect is, as Coleridge has excellently put it,
dazzling. But this highly ornate manner often gives
place to a style that is rigorously plain and simple,
and this latter is apt to decline to the pedestrian. It
does so decline, too often, in what the reader then
comes to regard as the interminable prolongation of
The Great Exemplar. Indeed, to be plain, the excessive length of the book is to-day its principal, and
perhaps its hopeless, fault.

This was not a fault at the time of its composition.
In the middle of the seventeenth century, people preferred their books of entertainment to be of immense
length. The kind of popular literature which Jeremy
Taylor directly challenged in *The Great Exemplar* was
the heroic novel recently introduced from France. In
his prison, Charles I. was now reading the *Cassandra*
of Calprenède, a romance in no fewer than twenty-
three volumes. Dorothy Osborne, in these same years,
was making lists of the lovers in the interminable
Almahide, and in the elephantine *Grand Cyrus* of Mlle de
Scudéry. Hitherto these huge books had been chiefly
read in French, but the tide of translation was beginning to set in. *Polexandre* had been published in
English in 1647, and *Artamenes* was shortly to follow,
in six colossal folio volumes. Bulk and prolixity were

---

[1] Mercy-seat.

no disadvantages in that age of the Commonwealth, when Puritan asceticism had sealed up the sources of genial enjoyment. In the country all festivities and sports had been abolished; in the town, with edicts of vindictive ferocity, all play-houses and places of amusement had been closed. The only entertainment left was literature, and people could not have it too elaborately prolonged. Yet even Jeremy Taylor, except in one notable instance, was never again so inordinately lengthy.

His holy romance, since he permits us to style it so, was eminently successful. But it did not pass entirely without attack. Jeremy Taylor, the most ingenuous of writers, was impudently accused of a literary fraud. It was asserted that his book was not his own, but merely translated from a folio *Vita Jesu Christi*, printed at Paris in 1509, by Ludolphus of Saxony. There seems to be always somebody ready to embark on these Shandean investigations, eager "to pluck my mother's thread-paper out of Slawkenbergius' book." Ludolphus, even in those days, cannot have been an author of easy reference, but a century and a half later Heber succeeded in discovering him, and allayed suspicion. "It is scarcely possible," Heber says, "to find two books written on any one subject which have so few coincidences of arrangement, sentiment, or expression." Deeply imprinted in the human breast is the desire to prove that every work was not written by its own author but by another man. Those who are convinced that all the poetry and drama in our literature was the composition of Bacon, should not pause until they have proved that all our theology was written by Ludolphus of Saxony.

A deep serenity of spirit is the key-note of *The Great Exemplar;* but it is not fantastic to read in the eighth section of the first part, where a curious effect of alarm and agitation is produced, a record of Taylor's feelings in the midst of the revolt of 1648. He speaks of the signs of the times, "no sermons there but when solitude is made popular, and the city moves into the wilderness; no comforts of a public religion, or visible remonstrances of the communion of saints. Of all the kinds of spiritual mercy, only one can there properly be exercised, and of the corporeal none at all." But, as he presently remembers, "the passions of the sensitive soul are like an exhalation," and when the danger had passed by, his peace returned. The first part of *The Great Exemplar* is dedicated, in terms of unimpaired affection, to Lord Hatton of Kirby, but this is almost the last occasion on which we meet the name of this nobleman in our narrative. Already in August 1648 he had withdrawn to Paris, where he began by keeping open house for the *émigrés,* but soon fell into poverty, and suffered a degradation of character from which he never recovered. So long as his son Christopher remained at Newton Hall School, this would be a link between Taylor and his former patron.

A persistent legend connects Jeremy Taylor with the last hours of Charles I. One of his descendants possesses a watch said to have belonged to the king; and two diamonds and a ruby, set in a ring, which are now in New York, are supposed to be royal gifts made on the road to execution. We are told, also, of "a few pearls and rubies which had ornamented the ebony case in which the king kept his Bible." Without

throwing any doubt upon the authenticity of these
relics, it may be observed that Charles I. may have
presented them to his former chaplain on various and
less tragic occasions than that of his death. It is
difficult to find room for Jeremy Taylor at that last
memorable scene. On the 23rd of December 1648,
Charles was conveyed from Hurst Castle, closely
guarded, to Windsor. It is possible that certain friends
might be smuggled in to take their leave of him before
the 19th of January, when he was brought up to St.
James's Palace. But up to the latter date, Charles
had not arrived at such a realisation of his fate as
would lead him to divide his possessions into keep-
sakes. After it, and up till the fatal 30th, even Juxon
and Herbert could scarcely pass through the rude
guard of soldiers, smoking and drinking in the very
precincts of the king's bedroom. One of the objects
mentioned above is said to bear the date, August 1647.
This, we have been recently told, "is evidently too
early." It appears to me, on the contrary, the date
most easy to reconcile with history. In August 1647
the king was at Putney, permitted to see his friends,
in comparative liberty and comfort. He had a few
weeks previously been reading *Liberty of Prophesying*
with extreme interest, and had been unable on all
points to coincide with the views expressed in it. He
naturally may have wished to discuss it with its
author. For the moment, everything was quiet in
South Wales; for the moment, Cromwell was anxious
to indulge and conciliate Charles. No conjectural
date for the last meeting between Jeremy Taylor and
his royal master seems to offer less difficulty than this
legendary one of August 1647. But that he went up

to London early in 1649, partly to carry the manuscript of *The Great Exemplar* to the publishers, and partly to see Juxon, Duppa, and other friends, is highly probable. He is said to have been consulted about the king's papers, and to have suggested the title of the *Eikon Basilike*.

CHAPTER III

(1650–1653)

THE retreat into which Jeremy Taylor had now with-drawn, under conditions the most fortunate which his genius could have desired, is situated in a part of South Wales, which is now very beautiful, and which there is reason to believe was then more beautiful still. Golden Grove was a large house, standing in its own undulating park, on the south side of the Towey, but about a mile from that river. It looked across the valley to a still lovelier and more romantic estate, Dynevor Castle. It was a little to the east of Grongar Hill, and shared the view which Dyer described some seventy years later in his famous poem, being situated in the midst of that

> " long and level lawn,
> On which a dark hill, steep and high,
> Holds and charms the wandering eye ;
> Deep are his feet in Towey's flood,
> His sides are clothed with waving wood ;
> And ancient towers crown his brow,
> That cast an awful look below."

This was the scene which rose before Jeremy Taylor every morning, as he left Golden Grove, struck north-ward across the meadows, crossed the winding Towey

at some fording-place or by the bridge to Llangathen,
and ascended, past the ruin which Dyer describes,
round

> " Whose ragged walls the ivy creeps,
>   And with her arms from falling keeps,"

on his way to the school-house at Newton Hall.

The ancient market-town of Llandilovawr was some
three miles off to the north-east, and from it, skirting
the palings of Golden Grove park, ran the high road
south to Llanelly.   At that time the valley of the
Towey seems to have been richly wooded, though later
on the timber was destroyed, and re-plantation was so
neglected, that late in the eighteenth century it bore
a very naked aspect.   In the period when Jeremy
Taylor lived there, the whole surroundings of Golden
Grove must have been romantic in the extreme, and
their delicate and picturesque beauty was in perfect
harmony with his florid genius.   No doubt, in his
day, the

> " woods, where echo talks,
>   The gardens trim, the terrace-walks,
>   The wildernesses, fragrant brakes,
>   The gloomy bowers and shining lakes "

of the Towey valley were, if possible, still more enchanting than when Dyer sang of them in the dawn
of the naturalistic revival.

The church of Llanfihangel-Aberbythych, where
Taylor's friend, Nicholson, ministered, stood at the
western confines of the park, and was but a few
minutes' distance from the rooms placed at Taylor's
disposal at the mansion.   Here, with his school and
his ministrations in the great house, and with long
talks with a few wise friends, Taylor lay protected

from the world for many happy years, surrounded
by every innocent pleasure, and left to the unbroken
cultivation of his eloquence and his fancy. It is to
this beautiful retreat, in a rich valley of South Wales,
that we owe the ripest products of his intellect. The
stamp of the physical beauty which surrounded him is
imprinted upon the best and happiest of his writings,
and we may say that Jeremy Taylor was nourished by
the Muses in the park of Golden Grove, as the goat-
herd Comatas was fed with honey by the bees while he
lay imprisoned in his master's cedarn chest.[1]

The conditions of Taylor's life at Golden Grove,
his extremely sequestered habits, the narrow circle in
which he laboured during so many years, his direct
responsibility as private chaplain to the lord and lady
of the place, give us authority to treat as autobiographical certain phrases in the books which he wrote in
Wales, which, if he had lived in the world of London,
or in a wide and uncritical society elsewhere, might
be taken as conventional. For instance, when he says
that every truly pious man "sets apart some solemn
time every year, in which, for the time quitting all
worldly business, he may attend wholly to fasting and
prayer, and the dressing of his soul by confessions,
meditations, and attendances upon God," it is obvious
that he must himself have made such an annual retreat
his practice, or any one of the few inhabitants of Llanfihangel-Aberbythych could have charged him with inconsistency. There is the same evidence that he was

---

[1] A rough engraving of Golden Grove adorns the 1657 edition of
the *Polemical Discourses*. The house was entirely burned down in
1729. In 1816 an avenue of trees in the park was still traditionally
known as Jeremy Taylor's Walk.

in the habit, several times during the day, of slipping
aside to "make frequent colloquies or short discoursings
between God and his own soul," on which occasions,
as we know that he did not approve of extempore
prayer, he certainly made use of some of the innumerable short "devotions" which form so considerable a
part of his published writings. Again, when he speaks,
not once or twice, of the advantage of getting out of
bed "sometimes" so as "to see the preparation which
the sun makes when he is coming forth from his
chambers of the east," it is hardly unreasonable to feel
assured that these remarks reflect one of his personal
habits. These little touches must not be pushed too
far, but they help to build up for us a portrait of the
man.

The earliest literary exercise on which Jeremy Taylor was occupied after the death of the king was a
practical work on conduct, almost a technical directory
or manual, the celebrated *Rule and Exercises of Holy
Living*. This was published in 1650, with a long title-
page explaining that the treatise dealt with "the means
and instruments of obtaining every virtue, and the
remedies against every vice, and considerations serving
to the resisting all temptations, together with prayers
containing the Whole Duty of a Christian," a summary
which neatly defines the contents of the volume. It is
not very easy to speak critically of this famous book,
which is certainly the best known of all Taylor's works,
and that which represents his thought and language
most directly to the majority of readers. It has been
incessantly reprinted, and is to be found in most house-
holds where books of any gravity of composition are
admitted. So widely circulated is it, indeed, that its

form and tenor have without doubt tended to create
a certain notion of Jeremy Taylor's style and manner.
It is not easy, however, to find terms in which to acknowledge the value of the *Holy Living*, and yet to
deprecate its being taken as an example of the habitual
or of the best side of its author's writing. But it is
necessary to do this, and to insist on the defects of
the book.

These defects rise out of its practical merits. It
is a didactic guide to the holy life. It is above all
things technical. It is "fitted to all occasions, fur-
nished for all necessities"; it is a guide to perfection, a map of all the virtues pushed to their
most inaccessible altitude. The author admits no
excuse for any kind of frailty; he pleads throughout
for the most austere and lofty practice as if it were
easily to be obtained. His ideal saint walks in spotless
glory along the mountain-tops, stepping upon virgin
snow. In order to enhance this imaginary perfection,
the preacher treats all forms of human weakness with
disdain, admits no pardonable frailties, demands the
debt of law to be paid in full, to the last farthing. This
is a point of view which may lend itself to admirable
effects in the hands of a theological philosopher, but
this Jeremy Taylor was not. He was a very great
writer, but it will scarcely be pretended that he was a
great thinker. The scope of the *Holy Living* is one
peculiarly unfavourable to a writer of Taylor's genius.
It is essentially impersonal and objective; it is all
written from the outside, in general terms. But we
have already suspected, and we shall have abundant
opportunity of proving as we proceed, that Jeremy
Taylor's treatment of conduct is apt to be obvious,

trite, and starved unless he has occasion to enrich it
with the fruits of his own experience, or to colour it
with his own vision.   An impersonal work of Jeremy
Taylor, therefore, sinks immediately to the second
level in a critical survey, even although its practical
value, its "usefulness," may have kept it on the highest
level in the ordinary life of the Church.   Let us have
the courage to say it — high as the devotional value is
— the *Holy Living* cannot be regarded as one of its
author's principal contributions to literature.

It has, however, parts of great passion and beauty,
where the individual note is not lacking.   The dedication, for instance, is a piece of splendid invective, a
lamentation over the miseries which followed 1649, and
an implied denunciation of the men who caused them.
The author breaks out in a cry of angry grief : —

"I have lived to see religion painted upon banners, and
thrust out of churches, and the temple turned into a tabernacle, and that tabernacle made ambulatory, and covered with
skins of beasts and torn curtains, and God to be worshipped,
not as He is, the Father of our Lord Jesus, an afflicted Prince,
the King of sufferings, . . . but rather as the Lord of hosts."

But this wail presently dies away in resignation.
No man shall have reason to be angry with Taylor
"for refusing to mingle in his unnecessary or vicious
persecution."   He bows the head, he accepts retirement,
poverty, humiliation.   The note sinks deeper and
deeper.   He will neither strive nor cry.   In earlier
years he fought for his prince and for his church, but
what is there now left to contend about ?   Life is
empty and barren ; there is nothing to expect or to
fear.   He is no longer apprehensive, no longer hopeful ;
the king is dead, the bishops are dishonoured, the

Church degraded.   What is there left to struggle for,
since the game is up ?   In this mood he prefers to lay
down a clear creed and directory for conduct.   In the
new naked era which has set in, men are bewildered
how to live.   He will draft regulations for behaviour
after the flood, for men who crowd back to the village
only to find priest and altar, bell and prayer-book,
swept away.   We shall not appreciate the appeal
which the *Holy Living* made to Anglican minds, if we
do not recognise the fierce and ironical resignation of
its despairing, royalist preface.

Of the general plan of the treatise, it must be said
that it has the formal defects of all such cut-and-dried
formularies, but especially of those of the seventeenth
century.   Its four main chapters deal with holiness,
and how to practise and maintain it; with sobriety
under five or six heads; with justice, — a chapter
which has been praised as a specimen of " casuistry in
its highest and noblest sense "; and with the duties of
religion.   The great difficulty which lies before those
who unreservedly praise the *Holy Living* is the lack
of clear reasoning in the mind of the author.   He is
eloquent about the vices, but rather vague and ineffective in his definitions of those which do not particularly
assail him.   It is amusing to see how very sensible and
cautious he is in his treatment of excessive indulgence
in the pleasures of the table.   Lord Carbery, one is
tempted to believe, was something of a gourmand.   It
must be remembered, if this criticism should seem to
be touched with flippancy, that all the directions for the
conduct of life were bound to be either entirely vague,
or else marked with a curious precision, in consequence
of the author's office as private chaplain in a great

house, isolated from the rest of mankind. Hence, the extreme looseness and indefiniteness of his diatribes against temptations which were not likely to fall in the way of his small circle of auditors.

Nor, in this connection, must we pass without one word of discrimination over the section on carnal voluptuousness, which he found it proper to include. Even as compared with the language of other seventeenth-century theologians, who were anything but mealy-mouthed, Taylor here is disagreeably broad and rough. It is useless to deny, what is an historical fact, that this part of his book has been a stumbling-block to hundreds of readers. Taylor was conscious, himself, that his treatment of this delicate theme would be distasteful to many, and might possibly give offence. He apologises for it, and his apology is not happy; he says: —

"If any man will snatch the pure taper from my hand and hold it to the devil, he will only burn his own fingers, but shall not rob me of the reward of my care and good intention."

This shows that he had been inclined, and perhaps advised, to omit or to modify his expressions. It is a pity that he did not act on the suggestion, for these paragraphs do not make for edification. Nor can a reader to-day forbear gently reminding Jeremy Taylor of what he has himself to say, so wisely and liberally, on this question of discretion, in the sermon called "The Good and Evil Tongue." It needs a sterner satirist or else a more human and pitiful moralist than he was to deal successfully with so very embarrassing a matter. But the section was needed in his formal

scheme, and he felt obliged to include it. In the
course of a chapter which we may be disposed to regret, however, occurs a mystical paragraph about vir-
ginity which we should have been unwilling indeed to
spare : —

> " Virginity is a life of angels, the enamel of the soul, the
> huge advantage of religion, the great opportunity for the re-
> tirements of devotion, and, being empty of cares, it is full of
> prayers."

From another passage in the same chapter, we learn
for the first time that Jeremy Taylor was a believer in
the possibility of contemporary witchcraft.

A literary feature which is very strongly marked in
the *Holy Living* is the author's dependence at this time
on the poets of antiquity. His arguments against the
vices are often taken, for pages together, entirely from
the Latin and Greek classics, and sometimes a charming turn is given to a phrase borrowed straight from
Æschylus or Martial. The systematic evolution of his
theme, divided in the provoking seventeenth-century
manner into heads and numbered paragraphs — which
Sir William Cornwallis, in his *Essays*, had amusingly
described as "the divisions that neat scholars use to
tie up the breeches of an argument or an oration with,"
— disturbs the reader's pleasure, and we are not
troubled to charge the preacher with inconsistency
when he throws this tiresome apparatus away, or
forgets it for a while, as in the noble apostrophe on
divine love in the fourth chapter, or that on content-
edness in the second chapter, where we come upon
enchanting Horatian phrases, in the author's true
manner, such as : —

" Corn from Sardinia, herds of Calabrian cattle, meadows through which pleasant Liris glides, silks from Tyrus, and golden chalices to drown my health in, are nothing but instruments of vanity or sin, and suppose a disease in the soul of him that longs for them, or admires them."

He does not divide his subject very consistently, and falls into illogical overlappings and repetitions of it, which sometimes suggest such patchwork as we have noted, though there carried out with far greater skill, in *The Great Exemplar*. Towards the end of the treatise, Taylor inveighs again very strongly against the efficacy of death-bed repentances, an attitude which was frequently to recur in his writings, and to awaken much animadversion. Finally, he adds to the treatise, and closes with, an essay which is evidently of independent composition, a grave and harmonious preparation to the receiving of the Holy Sacrament. Such in its variegated literary aspect is the *Holy Living*, a treatise to which, from the purely intellectual and artistic points of view, certain exceptions have to be made, but which has been used for edification by pious churchmen for two hundred and fifty years.

The sequestered stillness of Jeremy Taylor's life was now to be broken in upon by some tragical events. It is evident that a very warm feeling of mutual esteem had grown up between the divine and his patron's wife. Frances, Countess of Carbery, was the "tender providence that shrouded him under her wings," and her wisdom, goodness, and practical ability had come to be the mainstays of his fortune. This prop was removed by her sudden death at Golden Grove, on the 9th of October 1650. The atmosphere of Oxhey, where she was brought up, had been con-

templative and intellectual; her training was strict and
austere; and we are told, although the exact meaning
of these words is doubtful, that "God had provided a
severe and angry education to chastise the forward-
nesses of a young spirit and a fair fortune." She married Lord Carbery in June 1637, being very youthful
at the time. At the date of her death she was still *in
flore ætatis,* probably not more than two or three and
thirty years of age. Whatever vicissitudes her early
life may have suffered, her career at Golden Grove
seems to have been tranquil and pleasant enough. She
was very clever and tactful; a *placens uxor,* she had an
excellent influence over her husband, who adored her;
she was a charming talker, and eminently easy of
access — *conversationis suavissimæ.* As her years advanced, she became more remarkable for "severity,
modesty, and close religion," and of so exquisite a
moral delicacy that "you might as well have suspected
the sun to smell of the poppy that he looks on, as
that she could have been a person apt to be sullied by
the breath of a foul question." Her constitution was
undermined by a too constant burden of child-bearing.
During her brief married life, she brought into the
world ten children, of whom eight survived her, and
from the bed of her latest daughter, Althamia, she
never rose again. It appears that she had an intuition of her approaching end, and she told Jeremy
Taylor, before Althamia was born, that she had to
"go a great way in a little time," and must trim her
lamp and be ready to depart.

Accordingly, long before there was any sign of
mortal weakness of body, Lady Carbery, having "a
strange secret persuasion that the bringing this child

should be her last scene of life," passed through a paroxysm of terror, which presently gave way to resignation, except when she thought that her death might be attended with agonising pain, of which she had a constitutional dread. Her fears passed away, however, and the birth of her child was normal; but she never regained her strength, and faded painlessly out of life, merely shivering twice, as with " two fits of a common ague." Jeremy Taylor, who attended her in her last moments with spiritual consolation, wrote for her monument a long Latin inscription, and the following English portrait, which he calls a drawing in water colours : —

" She was . . . of a temperate, plain, and natural diet, without curiosity or an intemperate palate. She spent less time in dressing than many servants. Her recreations were little and seldom, her prayers often, her reading much. She was of a most noble and charitable soul; a great lover of honourable actions, and as great a despiser of base things. Hugely loving to oblige others, she was very unwilling to be in arrear to any upon the stock of courtesies and liberality. So free in all acts of favour, that she would not stay to hear herself thanked. . . . She was an excellent friend, and hugely dear to very many, especially to the best and most discerning persons ; to all that conversed with her, and could understand her great worth and sweetness. She was of an honourable, nice, and tender reputation ; and of the pleasures of the world, which were laid before her in heaps, she took a very small and inconsiderable share."

This passage is quoted from the *Funeral Sermon* which Taylor preached at her grave, and immediately published in quarto. This address was a model of its kind, and was widely circulated, finding admirers among the large public of those to whom Lady Carbery

was an object of no interest, but who accepted the
sermon as a piece of mortuary art, like the elaborate
verse-elegies for which several poets of a slightly
earlier age, but particularly Francis Quarles, had been
famous. The *Funeral Sermon at the Obsequies of the
Countess of Carbery* marks, however, an advance upon
the conventional type of elegy in prose and verse, in
that it offers no preposterous panegyric of the de-
ceased, but a reasonable and thoughtful enumeration
of her qualities. It took the form of a biography, and
we may note that it is the pattern upon which Rust
was closely to model his own invaluable tribute to its
author.

Taylor speaks with approbation of those " women of
noble birth and great fortunes" who "nurse their children, look to the affairs of the house, visit poor cottages,
and relieve their necessities, are courteous in the neighbourhood, learn in silence of their husbands or their
spiritual guides, read good books, pray often and speak
little," and devote themselves "to good housewifery
and charitable provisions for their family and neighbourhood." This was obviously a picture of the useful
and active life of the only "woman of noble birth and
great fortunes" whom his seclusion at Golden Grove
gave him an opportunity of observing. Nor does it
appear that, with these agreeable duties, Lady Carbery
combined the temper of a fanatic; she held it lawful
to relax and unbend the bow, like "St. John, who
recreated himself with sporting with a tame partridge,"
if we may believe Cassianus. On the whole, we have
a charming impression presented to us of the great lady,
whose mind and soul were so closely watched for some
five quiet years by her delicately appreciative chaplain.

When Lady Carbery died, Taylor was already engaged in a literary work of great importance, on which the character and enthusiasm of that admirable woman had put their stamp. We have noticed already, and shall have again to observe, a curious docility in the intellectual disposition of Jeremy Taylor, the result, perhaps, of a certain timidity, which usually demanded a stimulus from without to start him on an enterprise. We have already seen how much he owed to the initiation first of Laud and then of Lord Northampton; at Golden Grove it was evidently Lady Carbery who was his muse and his directing genius. Among other designs of her suggesting was that of a collection of his sermons, so arranged as to serve as a manual of piety for a whole year. This was a matter in which Taylor was slow to act; he was not sure that such a publication would be prudent or acceptable. But "the appetites of the hunger and thirst after righteousness" of that "dear lady, that rare soul," would brook no objections, and when she died, it was being prepared for the press.

Taylor immediately issued an instalment, in the form of *Twenty-eight Sermons preached at Golden Grove,* in 1651. This is the second or "Summer" half of the entire work, the first part of which, the "Winter" section, appeared in 1653; the two were united in all subsequent reprints, under the title of *Eniautos.*[1] This is the main storehouse or miscellany of Taylor's homilies. As we hold it, at present, however, the two parts are reversed from the original order of publication, and the history of the book thus obscured. Although Advent Sunday, of course, begins the eccle-

[1] That is to say, "A Year" (ἐνιαυτός).

siastical year, in dealing with the *Eniautos* we ought
to turn to the sermon for Whitsunday, and to consider
that the collection begins there. It is important, too,
to read first the dedication to the " Summer " half, and
to bear in mind that it refers to events which were
more than two years earlier than those dealt with in
what is now the opening address. If we do this, we
see that in 1651 Jeremy Taylor published his *Twenty-
eight Sermons,* as a legacy due to Lord Carbery from his
countess, but reluctantly, timidly, almost despairingly.
He expected no praise for them ; he feared that their
publication could little serve his reputation. By often
reading over and revising these essays, the pleasure
which he took in their composition had all evaporated.
He had " begun to grow weary and displeased " with
his own oratory, and he was very doubtful whether it
would either please or edify others.

Part of this was due to physical depression of spirits,
no doubt; part of it to the excessive disappointment
caused by the sudden removal of her for whom he had
prepared the work, and to whom he had looked forward as its earliest and most ardent reader. But it
was an attitude too complex and too unusual to be
easily explained. This was far from being the customary pose of the seventeenth-century divine, whether
he was Presbyterian or Jansenist, English or French.
As a rule no shadow of a suspicion that his publication
could be unwelcome to the pious agitated the Boanerges
of the moment. Not to welcome his sermons was to
show how gravely you were in need of them. But
Jeremy Taylor was not like the clamorous Rutherfords
on the one hand; nor on the other was he like such
fashionable preachers as Massillon, who, in telling Mlle

de Scudéry about the sermons he was preparing for the press, assured her that when she read them she would fancy herself listening to St. Augustine or to St. Bernard. It is curious that a collection of addresses more magnificent than any which a theologian of the English Church had hitherto addressed to the world should appear with the painful and faltering dedication of the *Twenty-Eight Sermons* of 1651.

But there were reasons for Taylor's reluctance. He was afraid of the results of withdrawing the personal element. These addresses had been written for and delivered in the presence of a very small cluster of peculiarly refined and highly-cultivated persons, who had a strong admiration for the preacher. Jeremy Taylor had been flattered for his delivery, for his address, doubtless for his golden voice and his angelic aspect, since compliments were not stinted in those days. He had been praised " as you should crown a conqueror with a garland of roses, or a bride with laurel." He had, by all testimony, what Bossuet defines as " une éloquence vive et impétueuse qui entraînait " those who listened, and entranced them. And he was carried on himself, and felt the Delphic fumes in his brain. But it is one thing to make great music " unto a little clan," and another to address, in cold print, the world at large. Taylor, in his delicate hermitage, shrank from the idea of a publicity which might wound him.

His orthodoxy, too, might be called in question, and, a little later on, it was. He would not care much for what the Parliamentarian divines would say, but the criticism of men like Duppa and Sheldon, his own friends and fellow-sufferers, made him anxious. There

was, for instance, his disbelief in the efficacy of
death-bed repentance, which was becoming a sort of
fanaticism with him.   There were other matters, some
of which will come before us in the course of this
inquiry, although the nature of it is literary and not
theological, in which Taylor held and was obliged con-
scientiously to advance views not shared by the rest
of the High Church clergy of his time.   He would
naturally be nervous lest these should lead to controversy, for which, at the moment, his mood particularly disinclined him.

A profound respect for the limitations and apparatus of religious oratory is strongly marked in these
sermons.   Jeremy Taylor was distinguished from
those English preachers who had most prominently
preceded him in that he was in no sense an impro-
visatore.   His best sermons — those which we possess
in the completed *Eniautos* — are composed with extreme care; on every page they bear evidence of the
long delays of art.   His own injunctions to those who
preach dwell on the need of competency, of labour,
of deliberation.   It is important to observe that he
arrived at the full stature of his genius at a moment
when the English Church had no need of a Tertullian.
In 1651 no obligation lay upon one of the hunted
ministers of a fallen Episcopacy to strike at such
vices as ambition, or gallantry, or the greed of gold.
What was wanted, in that melancholy hour, was a
physician of souls, one who had the skill to comfort
the racked nerves and pour oil into the aching wounds
of the Church.   This precisely suited the temperament
of Jeremy Taylor, who was nothing of a pontiff and
nothing of a satirist, but whose seraphic gentleness

exhaled itself in the deep and comfortable balms of consolation.

Accordingly, in the *Sermons* of Taylor we find a studied avoidance of the fury of the preachers of an earlier time. All is in the spirit of St. Chrysostom; these are *aurea dicta.* His acquaintance with the human heart inspired homilies which were addressed, not to indifferent or hostile listeners, but to those who were greedy of pious counsel. He advances to his task with tact, with insinuation, with an energetic imagery which will fetter a refined fancy and uplift it. In those days the sermon was beginning to be a literary instrument, and Taylor bends his genius to use it so as to correct bad taste as well as bad morals. His *Sermons* give a curious impression of cosmopolitan distinction. He constantly introduces a phrase, — such as " we walk by the obelisk, and meditate in piazzas, that they that meet us may talk of us," — which seems in a moment to lift us completely out of the provincial environment of the ordinary Anglican divine of the period. And Taylor does this without falling, on the other hand, into the affectation of the " pretty sermon," into that rainbow-coloured Marinism which was all the mode in London, and of which Anthony à Wood has preserved ridiculous examples. Taylor's appeal to the conscience is always direct, and he throws his art, the unequalled beauty of his style, into the presentment of dogma, with a passion of strenuous piety.

So, for instance, when we read, in " The Faith and Patience of the Saints " : —

" Jesus was like the rainbow, which God set in the clouds as a sacrament to confirm a promise and establish a grace. He was half made of the glories of the light, and half of the

moisture of a cloud. In His best days, He was but half
triumph and half sorrow " —

the incomparable melody and delicacy of the phrase
must no more be condemned as the screen of a conceit
than must one of Shakespeare's unusual and penetrating turns. It is beautiful, but it is true as well;
it bears thinking about; it illuminates, it does not
astonish and obscure the idea by the glare of false
ornament.

The splendour of these *Twenty-Eight Sermons* is very
striking. In no work of Jeremy Taylor's are there
to be found so many images taken from light and
colour and living creatures on the wing. He exercises
every legitimate art of finished literary oratory, from
the abrupt beginning, " And lose his own soul ? " or
" This is the epicure's proverb ! " to the solemn and
stately close. The curious reader will find that he almost
invariably ends in a studied verbal harmony. Between
these two extremes there is an infinite, but carefully
balanced, variety of treatment. He is always endea-
vouring to appeal to his auditors' common sense, to
touch them by images from nature, by analogies from
contemporary life. He is always careful to give a
tangible form, if possible, to his abstract ideas, by
a metaphor, or an illustration. Each of these sermons
occupied about three-quarters of an hour in tranquil
delivery, some a little less, none more than an hour.
And this may lead us to a consideration of a point
which has been frequently raised, For whom were
these elaborate works of art intended ?

It has been suggested that discourses as finished in
form as those which Bossuet was, a decade later, to
pronounce before the Court of Louis XIV. could not

have been composed for a circle of acquaintances in a
Welsh country-house. Heber himself acceded to this,
and being confronted with the plain statement that
Taylor's *Eniautos* was "preached at Golden Grove,"
started the theory, which has been generally accepted,
that in preparing his sermons for the press he materi-
ally changed them from "what he had delivered to
his rustic auditory in Wales," and that, as so delivered,
the ornamental and philosophical portions were omitted.
This I am by no means prepared to believe. First,
because the sermons, as they were printed, were not
longer, but decidedly shorter, than was the custom
with such compositions, and secondly, because the
"ornament" and "philosophy" are not of a nature
which could be detached, but make a part of the
integral texture. Moreover, no Welsh-speaking "rustic
auditory" would be present in the private chapel of
Golden Grove, but primarily the lord and lady of the
place, with their pronounced appetite for the refine-
ments of theological literature, and secondarily the
other clergy from Newton Hall, and such neighbouring gentry as, in their religious isolation, would drive
over in their equipages from distant parts of the
country to be thus refreshed and delighted.

To a discreet and enthusiastic auditory of this kind,
the *Eniautos* would not sound too academical. It might
even seem too popular. The recondite nature of the
allusions would not appear excessive to persons accustomed to hear long passages of Greek and Latin recited
from the fathers. Heber himself has noted that of
Pococke, although one of the first scholars of the day,
it was slightingly complained in his parish that,
"though a kind and neighbourly man, he was no

Latinist," simply because he preached in homely English. Jeremy Taylor seems, on more than one occasion, to express a certain apprehension of a similar blame. In his case, it might arise, however, not so much from his neglect of the patristic authorities as from his extraordinary fondness .or dissolving little crystals of such very profane writers as Martial, Catullus, and Petronius in his holy discourse. Of this no more curious example can be pointed to than the way in which he has (in "The Spirit of Grace") built up a most brilliant summary of the mysteries of our faith on a basis so little to be anticipated as a tag from an ode of Anacreon.

If the shock of Lady Carbery's death, striking "more suddenly than upon the poor slave that made sport upon the theatre," deeply affected Taylor's spirits, they were still further depressed by a blow which came even closer to him. Absolutely no light has hitherto been thrown on the movements of the wife whom he had married at Uppingham early in 1639, but she had probably joined her husband at Llanfihangel in 1645. Their eldest child, William, had died at Uppingham in 1642; five others had come in rapid succession. The allusions to Mrs. Taylor, which can without overbold conjecture be traced in writings of her husband, are few. But there can be no doubt that she is the "affectionate wife" whom Taylor tenderly recalls, who,

" when she hath been in fear of parting with her beloved husband, heartily desired of God his life or society upon any conditions that were not sinful, and chose to beg with him rather than to feast without him ; and the same person hath upon that consideration borne poverty nobly, when God hath heard her prayer in the other matter."

It may be that Mrs. Taylor's health suffered a slow decline, for references to the burden of illness in a house, and its attendant fatigues and anxieties, are frequent in her husband's writings at this period. In a passage where the inconveniences of their poverty are plainly referred to, he adds, "sickness doth so often embitter the content of a family." It seems probable that the parents were not entirely of one mind about the education of children. In the *Holy Dying* he speaks with strange severity of the bad influence of mothers on their children : —

"These soften them with kisses and imperfect noises, with the pap and breast-milk of soft endearments. They rescue them from tutors, and snatch them from discipline ; they desire to keep them fat and warm, and their feet dry and their bellies full ; and then the children govern, and cry, and prove fools and troublesome, so long as the feminine republic does endure."

The modern reader will be all with Mrs. Taylor in this matter, and will surmise that if "the bold and valiant" divine had taken more pains to see that his little children's feet were dry, the dreadful mortality that presently pursued them might have been averted. But Jeremy Taylor is himself too human to be quite consistent, and in other places commends the physical care of little children.

News of the death of Phœbe Taylor is preserved for us in a curious way, in a piece of a letter which has been torn across. It was written, on the 1st of April 1651, to Sir William Dugdale, the antiquary ; what remains of it is of deep interest. Among other things, Taylor says, " I have but lately buried my dear wife." He also mentions, " I have some things

now in [   ] preparing, *The Rule of Holy Dying ;*
I have [   ]ow transcribing it." The book, of
which the first draft is here mentioned, was completed
and sent to the press in October of the same year, the
dedication being signed on the anniversary of Lady
Carbery's death. It was adorned with a folding plate
by Peter Lombart, representing the hall of a country
house, where a clergyman displays the life-sized picture
of a skeleton to a handsome lady, with her husband and
child. This group is supposed to contain portraits
of Taylor himself and of the Carberys. In the dedication addressed to the Earl, Taylor speaks with dignity
of their common bereavement; "both your lordship
and myself have lately seen and felt such sorrows of
death, and such sad departure of dearest friends, that
it is more than high time we should think ourselves
nearly concerned." Death had come so near them
both as to fetch away a portion from their very hearts,
and a community of grief drew the survivors together
in a solemn and pious bond.

The praise, which it was not possible to give to
the *Holy Living* without reserve, will be withheld by
no competent critic from *The Rules and Exercises of
Holy Dying*. The resemblance between these two
treatises, which are often confounded, is a purely superficial one. Considered as literature, the superiority
of the latter over the former is immense; since that
genius which is only fitfully and feebly apparent in
the *Holy Living*, illuminates the *Holy Dying* in a
limpid and continuous glory. Between the two
volumes there is all the difference which there must
be between a piece of task-work, honestly and compe-
tently performed, and a product of vehement inspira-

tion. Jeremy Taylor had formed no project of a continuation of the *Holy Living*. On the contrary, that work had included meditations and prayers to be used at the approach of death. But now Taylor had himself passed through the crisis of watching the demise of a beloved and sentient being; he had passed through this crisis twice in a few months. It was no longer a question of conventional piety, of what all Christians felt or should feel at this extraordinary juncture; it was an observation of what his own heart had throbbed with in agony and terror and incurable regret. In the coldness of his own hearth-stone, in the like coldness at Golden Grove, he sat down and wrote one of the most beautiful prose compositions of the seventeenth century, a threnody palpitating with enthusiasm and emotion.

Jeremy Taylor claimed that the *Holy Dying* was the earliest work of its kind "that I remember to have been published in the Church of England." He admits that there had been many in the Church of Rome, but he holds the resemblance of his treatise with these to be quite superficial. He claims an originality; "in this affair I was forced almost to walk alone"; the only help he has had having come from the fountains of Scripture and from "some experience in the cure of souls." This, then, is the first point which it may be useful to consider in dealing with the causes of the vitality of the *Holy Dying* as a work of art. Its brilliant freshness is owing, in the outset, to the fact that the author is not, like so many theologians of his time, chewing the cud of the old accepted platitudes and holy saws, but is feeding the arteries of his imagination with a constant flow of recent personal observation. These are clinical notes, sharply perceived in protracted hours of acute mental activity; and they are used to produce a sort of pathology of the soul in physical pain. He has evidently been deeply impressed by the experiences of these dear persons in their hour of agony, by their "unequal courages and accidental fortitude." Being brought face to face, in this way, with all the violence of death, he is at once fascinated and exalted by it. He fears a kind of hysterical reaction from what he has endured and seen, and he determines to use his emotion for a purpose at once creative and sedative, because "nothing is more unreasonable than to entangle our spirits in wildness and amazement, like a partridge in a net, which she breaks not, though she breaks her wings."

Few points are more interesting than the modernness of Taylor's attitude to many themes which were still in his time subjected to the traditions of the Renaissance. The conception of death which prevailed in the poetry, the sermons, and the philosophy of the early part of the seventeenth century was a survival of the "Danses Macabres" of the fifteenth and sixteenth. Death was still generally regarded anthropomorphically and positively, as a great pale tyrant, an executioner, a headsman concealed behind a curtain. He was "the unsparing pursuivant with eagles' wings"; he was even the grisly, cynical humorist, waiting to pounce on the king as he ascends his throne, or to strike down the beggar as he reels out of the tavern. In literature, this sentiment of death as the skeleton that hides to take his victim unawares, because, if met in front, he might be parleyed with and even tricked,

had produced some magnificent apologies and outbursts. It had lent a wing to the heavy, historic muse
of Ralegh; it had spread its velvet over the sermons
of Donne; it had inspired a choir of doleful lyrists.
But it was cast out of court, and relegated to a place
among things childish and outworn, by the *Holy Dying*
of Jeremy Taylor, and never again could this conception of death, as a gymnastic skeleton with a dart
springing from the tomb, be put forward without
danger of awakening a smile of disgust.

To the elegists of a decayed Renaissance, death
had seemed a sort of central actor in a tragedy. To
Taylor, as to a physician of to-day, it is not a figure
at all, but a negation; a state in which the powers of
movement and assimilation have ceased their activity, a
point where the equilibrium in which life has consisted
has broken down, and where what is left is nothing.
Taylor's originality consists in the firmness with which
he turns away from the conception of a grinning shape
behind the arras, ready to strike, and concentrates his
attention on the psychology of the still living, but
rapidly declining and obscured humanity. Accordingly
he does not, in the manner of his predecessors, expatiate
on the majesty of death, or cultivate the pretension
and splendour of high family funerals. In particular,
he has little or nothing to say about the subject which
had so deeply stirred the imagination of the previous
age, the conduct of obsequies. That does not interest him in the least. There is no dwelling upon
the deaths of great persons, a matter in which the
early seventeenth century had been so disagreeably
insistent. Jeremy Taylor finds the death of " a poor
shepherd or a maid-servant " quite as interesting as

that of a prince or a countess. And in an age so copious and tumultuous in its funerals, he is severe in denouncing anything like ambitious or pompous sorrow, and in deprecating all ostentatious lamentation for the dead.

Another very interesting example of the modernity of Taylor's mind, and his freedom from the trammels of his time, is to be observed in the curious notes on the approach and development of illness, and on the behaviour of those who surround the sick, in the later part of the *Holy Dying.* He seems to have divined, by sheer exercise of the imagination, some of the great truths of modern medicine, so far at least as to reject, or question, that universal idea of disease as the work of a malignant spirit outside the body, of which Sir Frederick Treves has lately spoken in his interesting strictures on a great physician younger than Taylor, Sir Thomas Browne of Norwich. Jeremy Taylor, in his closely observed notes on the psychology of persons attacked by sickness, seems to rise above the preternatural view, and to accept, with clairvoyance, the simple natural theory of the processes of dissolution. He even seems to have foreseen something of that very theory of the beneficence of some of the symptoms of disease which is claimed as a discovery almost of our own day. He points out the benefit of some illnesses in giving the nerves an opportunity of rest; sickness becoming "the more tolerable because it cures very many evils, and takes away the sense of all the cross fortunes which amaze the spirits of some men, and transport them beyond the limits of all patience." And he actually perceives that some acute forms of illness may be, as our great modern surgeon puts it, "the outcome of nature's vigorous effort to minimise the calamity," and force the patient to a recumbent posture, where, says the divine, "all losses and disgraces, domestic cares and public evils, . . . lie down and rest upon the sick man's pillow."

In the more enthusiastic parts of the *Holy Dying*, the sustained brightness and abundance of the style are extraordinary. The images bud and branch under our eyes in a miraculous profusion. To this work Jeremy Taylor brought a mind steeped in the loftiest poetry of antiquity; nowhere are the references so frequent as they are here to Lucretius, Horace, and Lucan, to Persius, Ovid, and Petronius Arbiter. Almost the only modern books which he quotes are the then very popular *Odes* of the Polish poet, Casimir, who had lately died, and the *Funeral Monuments* of John Weever, the antiquary. But although the ancients colour so much of the tissue of his style, he has now almost entirely abandoned the vexatious habit of quoting them in bulk. He has learned at last the very useful lesson which English prose had been so slow to learn, but which Joachim du Bellay had successfully taught the French authors a hundred years before — namely, that good masons do not build their new buildings partly of fresh brick, and partly of stones torn out of stately ancient houses, but leave what other men have built, and try to construct as beautifully as they did, in reverent imitation, but with a different material. An example, taken at random from the *Holy Dying*, may serve to exemplify Taylor's method. Here a tag from the *Hippolytus* of the pseudo-Seneca serves as the grain of sand around which the nacreous ingenuity of the English writer secretes its layers of mother-of-pearl : —

> " Since we stay not here, being people but of a day's abode,
> and our age is like that of a fly and contemporary with a
> gourd, we must look somewhere else for an abiding city, a
> place in another country to fix our house in, whose walls and
> foundation is God, where we must find rest, or else be restless
> for ever. For whatever ease we can have or fancy here is
> shortly to be changed into sadness or tediousness. It goes
> away too soon, like the periods of our life ; or stays too long,
> like the sorrows of a sinner. Its own weariness, or a contrary
> disturbance, is its load, or it is eased by its revolution into
> vanity and forgetfulness. And where either there is sorrow
> or an end of joy there can be no true felicity, which must be
> had by some instrument and in some period of our duration.
> We must carry up our affections to the mansions prepared for
> us above, where eternity is the measure, felicity is the state,
> angels are the company, the Lamb is the light, and God is the
> portion and inheritance."

Of all the writings of Jeremy Taylor, the *Holy Dying*
achieved the most direct and durable popularity.
Twenty authorised editions of it appeared before the
close of the seventeenth century. It produced an
instant effect in humanising the piety of English
readers, which controversy had bitterly exacerbated.
Taylor's attitude, his philosophy of action, was holy,
but it was neither morose, fanatical, nor uncharitable.
It was inspired by a gentle sobriety, a brooding
tenderness and pity. On some points it displayed an
extraordinary liberality, and in its melancholy it was
marvellously wholesome. The curious morbidity of
the age found no support in Taylor's healthy sweetness.

The dying are to be led to examine their conscience,
but not in gloom ; the scrutiny is not to be distracted
by the terrors of law and punishment. All this was

eminently serviceable to the irritated nerves of his contemporaries; it was a balm to their spiritual wounds.

We may hope that the success of this and other of his literary writings was of practical benefit to Taylor's fortunes, which were at a low ebb in 1651. In that year he was embarrassed by a cessation of the patronage of Lord Hatton. "I am troubled," he says, "that he will not honour me with a letter." He was doubtless unaware of the penury into which Lord Hatton had now sunk in Paris. He makes a very strong appeal to Lord Carbery's generosity in the dedication to the *Holy Living*, which book he compares, with more quaintness than propriety, to the gift of "a piece of gum or the fat of a cheap lamb." In the same work he seems to describe himself as "a little bee that feeds on dew or manna, and lives upon what falls every morning from the storehouses of heaven, clouds and providence." In the *Holy Dying* he is still more explicit, and speaks of the joy with which he ministers to the sick and penitent, "having scarce any other possibilities left me of doing alms, or exercising that charity by which we shall all be judged at doomsday." His salary as chaplain at Golden Grove must have been small, and perhaps irregularly paid.

It was possibly the opportunity to sell yet another manuscript to a London bookseller which led to the publication, in this same year, of a folio pamphlet entitled *Clerus Domini*. This is one of the rarest and most obscure of Taylor's writings, though copies of it are sometimes found bound up with the *Eniautos*. It was a relic of his old Oxford days, and had been written, some eight or nine years previously, at the special command of "our late king." So much had happened, so much had been overturned and ruined in the English Church since its composition, that it must have seemed obsolete to readers of 1651. It was issued without dedication or prefatory matter of any kind, perhaps surreptitiously. It is concerned with arguments for the ministerial order as an absolute religious necessity. The author asserts that the strictness and severity of the hierarchy are pleasing to God, and have descended to us directly from that primal Consecrator, the Holy Ghost. There must be experts in religion, as in art and science, men of careful training, supernaturally selected, by whose delicate and skilful care alone piety can escape being "bruised by the hard hand of mechanics."

The treatise is very outspoken, and must have been excessively distasteful to the Parliamentarian divines, if any of them came across it. It treats their pretensions with the utmost contempt. They are all presumptuous amateurs, who pretend to work a machine of the nature of which they are profoundly ignorant. Four great mysteries are defined as lying within the exclusive province of the consecrated minister: these are remission of sins, the preaching of the Gospel, baptism, and the distribution of the Sacrament. The minister is lifted above common humanity by his apostolical prerogative. He is ordained that he may bridge over the mysterious and wonderful chasm between God and man; this none but "a settled ministry" can do. The self-chosen presbyter or preacher has no apparatus for crossing the abyss, and his offers of ministration are as absurd as they are profane. This is the temper of Jeremy Taylor before his afflictions had mellowed him, and the chief interest of *Clerus Domini* is the evidence which it gives us of the advance of every species of liberality which he had made during his years of seclusion in Wales. It is quite possible that he had nothing to do with its publication in 1651, but that Royston acquired it from some one at Oxford in whose hands it had remained ever since Taylor's flight in 1644.

From a literary point of view *Clerus Domini* is almost valueless, except, to the reader who approaches his works in the order of their publication, as a startling instance of the development of Taylor's intellect and style since he came to Golden Grove. Here we have the tedious, constant quotation from the fathers in Latin and Greek, the equally tedious, casuistical building-up of a structure which seems like argument and is not, the clumsy sentences without felicity or music. Indeed, it would hardly be worth while to mention *Clerus Domini*, if it were not so useful a text upon which to discourse on the wonderful advance in all the powers of its author which followed his flight to Wales. The contrast may be still further emphasised by comparison of it with two compositions which appeared in the same year (1651), in a little book called *Choice Forms of Prayer*. This was the venture of a publisher who collected from a large number of popular divines the devotions which they were in the habit of using before and after preaching a sermon. Jeremy Taylor's contributions, particularly the first, are models of purity and grace.

For the next three years what we know of Taylor is almost exclusively confined to a record of his publications. His life seems to have become more and more sequestered. Rust speaks of his "solitude" and of his "retirement" at this time, and of his implicit

H

devotion to the composition of "those excellent discourses, which are enough of themselves to furnish a
library." During these years the only friend of whose
presence we are allowed to be conscious is Lord
Carbery, who seems to have preserved an even tenor
of protective sympathy. But Taylor was now in correspondence with theologians in various parts of the
kingdom. In a letter to Gilbert Sheldon, his old friend,
the former warden of All Souls College, Oxford, dated
April 11, 1653, he speaks of obtaining for a certain
manuscript treatise of his as much criticism from the
neighbouring Welsh clergy as he could ; and of a conference he has lately had "with a Jesuit in these parts."
The work which he mentions thus to Sheldon is the
Real Presence, of 1654, and he states that he has sent
a copy in proof-sheets to Dr. Brian Duppa, the aged
Bishop of Salisbury, who was now living a life of strict
retirement at Richmond in Surrey; this eminent divine
was another of the old All Souls friends of happier
times. We find Taylor thanking Sheldon, who has
done him the very welcome favour of paying him what
appear to be some partial arrears of his college stipend
— Taylor "resolving to take up the remaining portion
of the debt at the great Audit" — and sending him a
new edition of *The Great Exemplar* and his new volume
of *Sermons*.

The last-mentioned book, which Taylor refers to in
this letter to Sheldon as published before April 1653,
is perhaps, from a purely literary point of view, the
most important which he ever produced. It was issued
as *Twenty-Five Sermons preached at Golden Grove, being
for the Winter Half-Year,* and completes the series of
which the first instalment appeared in 1651. Like its

predecessor, it mainly consists of pairs of sermons, although in many cases there are groups of three, and there is one of four; but the entire *Eniautos* does not contain a single address which is complete in itself. It follows, therefore, that no effort is made to provide appropriate teaching for particular feast days, and, in fact, with the exceptions of Whitsuntide and Advent, no special or topical allusiveness is attempted. What has been already said in general about the sermons of Jeremy Taylor is true of this, his most magnificent collection of them. The dedication, once more to Lord Carbery, is a brilliant essay on the value of sermons. The author observes that "all the great necessities of the Church have been served by the zeal of preaching in public," which "restored the splendour of the Church, when barbarism and wars and ignorance, either sate in, or broke the doctor's chair in pieces." It is therefore peculiarly proper that in this dreadful age of heresy and schism, God's ministers should proclaim "those truths which are the enamel and beauty of our churches." There is no trace in this dedication of the reluctance and regret which marked that of 1651. In 1653 Taylor has no more diffidence. He knows now that he had a great and fruitful work to perform from the pulpit. This is an interesting psychological point which has not hitherto been observed by the successive editors who have reversed the order of the two sections of the *Eniautos*.

Again, in the body of the sermons, we are conscious, if we read them as they were written, of an important advance in the genius of the author. The *Twenty-Five* have all the lucidity and harmony of the *Twenty-Eight*, but they have in addition a certain sublimity of tone

which is unknown to the works which Taylor composed before the deaths of Lady Carbery and of his
wife. In some of these homilies he touches the very
highest level of human oratory. He proposes no new
theology, he discusses no spinosities of creed; he
maps the path of conduct, and enlightens it with all
the colour and radiance of his luminous experience.
In each sermon there comes the direct appeal to the
imagination of his auditors. The skill with which
he presents picture after picture to the eyes of the
listeners is wonderful. Let us take, for example, the
first sermon on "Christ's Advent." Here we are hurried from vivid scene to scene; in rapid succession
we watch the passage of the plague-cart through a
doomed city; we have a Michelangelesque presentment of the terrors of the Day of Judgment; we
watch a party of youths and girls carousing at the
wine-cup; we listen to a Greek philosopher address-
ing his disciples in an enclosure; we have the pathetic
drama of a young gentleman breaking from his ungodly
mother, with her repentance, and his backsliding, and
her ultimate reproaches; we are the spectators at a sun-
rise, and then at an earthquake on the shores of the
Mediterranean, and then at an apocalyptic scene when

"the birds shall mourn and change their songs to threnes
and sad accents. Rivers of fires shall rise from the east and
the west, and the stars shall be rent into threads of light, and
scatter like the beards of comets."

Nor does all this exhaust the variety of the preacher's
images, while this wealth of illustration and allusion
never interferes for a moment with the clear flow of
the orator's solemn evangelical argument.

In dealing with the mysteries of religion, it is interesting to see how completely Taylor continues master of his voice.   We see him in a sort of ecstasy; his fancy, with outspread wings, soars up into the empyrean, yet he retains it wholly under his control. Nowhere, in the series of his writings, does he deal with themes in which the enthusiastic cry of the preacher is so apt to break in a kind of hysterical falsetto as he does in the *Twenty-Five Sermons.*   Yet he remains always master of his art.   In his three great addresses on "Doomsday-Book" his reticence is extraordinary.   Here, where the temptation to expatiate on horror is so great, Taylor is careful to dwell more on the recompenses than on the punishments.   He shrinks from all those material catalogues of terrific experience in which the Mediæval theologians delighted.   He is loath to admit the doctrine of eternal torment, but leans to the kindlier hope that the wicked soul is broken up and destroyed, although he warns all those who still lie "in the neighbourhood and fringes of the flames of hell" not to trust to this.

In the different numbers of these sermons Jeremy Taylor sounds the whole diapason of majestic eloquence.   Nor does he neglect the craving of the ear for quieter periods and a more broken cadence.   The group of sermons on "The Return of Prayers" offers us instances, as many as we can desire, of both forms of beauty.   Here is a fragment in the more ornate manner: —

"Our prayers upbraid our spirits when we beg coldly and tamely for those things for which we ought to die, which are more precious than the globes of kings and weightier than imperial sceptres, richer than the spoils of the sea, or the treasures of the Indian hills.''

And here is a passage in which the short, nervous sentences are like those of our latest masters of colloquial English : —

"Holy prayer procures the ministry and service of angels. It rescinds the decrees of God. It cures sicknesses and obtains pardon. It arrests the sun in its course, and stays the wheels of the chariot of the moon. It rules over all God's creatures, and opens and shuts the storehouses of rain. It unlocks the cabinet of the womb, and quenches the violence of fire. It stops the mouths of lions, and reconciles our sufferance and weak faculties with the violence of torment and sharpness of persecution. It pleases God and supplies all our needs. But prayer, that can do this much for us, can do nothing at all without holiness, for God heareth not sinners, but if any man be a worshipper of God, and doth His will, him He heareth.''

There was no one else in England in 1653, there was no one to arise for a long time after that date, who could write sustained prose with this simplicity and force and delicate precision.

From this volume, in which the variety and fulness of Taylor's imagination are seen in their highest development, it is difficult to part ourselves. The whole *Eniautos* might take as its motto a phrase which occurs in one of its most beautiful sections, " The Marriage Ring": —

"These are the little lines of a man's duty, which, like threads of light from the body of the sun, do clearly describe all the regions of his proper obligations.''

The simplicity and gravity, the light and swiftness of Taylor's exhortations are all summed up in this paragraph, which includes even, if we look deep

enough, their humanity and their humanism. This last
deserves special notice. We can even trace with what
books the preacher had been refreshing his memory.
When he wrote "Apples of Sodom" his mind was
steeped in the *Hecuba* of Euripides; "The Marriage
Ring" testifies to his deep enjoyment of the Greek
Anthology; when he sat down to meditate on "Christian Simplicity," he had just been reading the third
book of Cicero's *Offices*. In this he is the greatest, as
he was the last, of the seventeenth century theologians
who took the picturesque parts of the classics as their
storehouse of allusion; in him a phase of the pure
Renaissance reaches its highest point. No one before
him had filled his pages with half so many images of
plastic beauty: in this he is in our prose what Spenser
had been in our poetry. And after him was to follow,
almost immediately, a generation blind alike to natural
phenomena and to the corporeal loveliness embodied
in ancient literature.

One curious omission will be noted in the sermons,
as in the other writings of Jeremy Taylor. The
absence of almost all allusion to the life of the poor
is very curious. Such references as we may discover
are perfunctory and vague. The teaching of Taylor
is in the main aristocratic; it is delivered from a
seraphic height, and addressed to all classes of men,
but particularly to those who are influential and well-
to-do. No temptation, no frailty of the rich is allowed
to pass unindicated or unreproved. The preacher is
speaking in the private chapel of a great house, and
mainly to those who are responsible from their wealth,
their intellect, or their influence. Outside are the
hordes of the wild Welsh, but of them the preacher

never speaks and never seems to think. The select
folk who came to Golden Grove to listen to him ate
sumptuously every day; their danger was to forget
God in their pleasures and in their indolence; and
the preacher reproves them, seeks to awaken their
consciences, draws them back to duty by such exquisite arts and appeals as would come most directly
home to their refinement. This involves, to be just,
no harsh judgment upon Jeremy Taylor, even in this
one particular, for he did exactly what it was his duty
to do. Yet we cannot help wishing that the demo-
cratic element in society had also had an opportunity
to attract him. It did not, and it was really not at
Golden Grove, but ten years later in the court of
Louis XIV., that this essentially modern note was
to be sounded. It was Bossuet, and not Taylor, who
was to introduce the definite consideration of the cause
of the poor, and to bid the Christian world listen to
the "cri de misère à l'entour de nous, qui devrait nous
fondre le cœur."

For ten years the current of Jeremy Taylor's life
had now been absolutely unbroken, except by the
hand of death. He had lived, almost as retired as
Moses in his cloud, in a sequestered valley of South
Wales, which was full of the sound of waters, and undisturbed by human voices. By a dispensation which
might easily have seemed miraculous, through the
cruellest time of distraction and peril, this exquisite
talent had been preserved intact, hidden as if in the
hollow of a mighty hand, granted every favourable
opportunity for growing to its full stature. Nothing
had been omitted which could enhance the advantages
of this hermitage, where there was poverty and yet

no want, leisure enough, and yet some healthful business, no crowd to distract and press, but a little circle
of auditors, sympathetic, earnest, and appreciative. In
this beautiful woodland, with a roll of the winding
Towey bent round him like an arm, Jeremy Taylor
had grown to be the greatest prose writer in England.
He had no rival among those who understood and
knew. It might well be that he was sometimes content to drop further struggle, and to look forward
with satisfaction to a quiet burial in the churchyard of
Llanfihangel. Like the prophet in Alfred de Vigny's
poem, he might cry: —

> " O Seigneur, j'ai vécu puissant et solitaire,
> Laissez-moi m'endormir du sommeil de la terre."

But this was not to be. A variety of circumstances,
without immediately severing his connection with
Golden Grove, was now to draw him out into the light
of common day, and cause him to take part in the
anxieties and afflictions of his fellow-men.

CHAPTER IV

(1654–1658)

JEREMY TAYLOR had enjoyed complete immunity at Golden Grove. No one had disturbed the growth of his soul. His genius had spread its branches and flowered like a magnolia under the shadow of a southern wall in a quiet courtyard. In that period of the cruel discomfiture of his friends, he alone was protected by his powerlessness, by the modesty of his fortunes. As he said himself, "No man goes about to poison a poor man's pitcher, nor lays plots to forage his little garden, made for the hospital of two bee-hives, and the feasting of a few Pythagorean herb-eaters." But when the poor man leaves his rosemary and his rue, and wanders forth into the market-place, he finds himself jostled by the throng, and may be can never recover his hermitage. This is precisely what happened to our divine, whom circumstances, or his own impatience, now tempted forth into the world, at first only on short visits, and then altogether, with the result that, lover of contemplation as he was, he never again knew what perfect security and perfect rest meant.

It is probable that for some time past he had been

106

in the habit of coming up to town whenever he was
about to publish a book. He seems to have been in
frequent personal contact with Royston, his publisher,
who is much less likely to have travelled down into
Carmarthenshire to see his client than to have offered
him hospitality in London. From 1654 onwards this
ceases to be a matter of conjecture; we find Jeremy
Taylor frequently going up to town, and light is
thrown upon his movements by his forming a new and
most valuable friendship, namely with John Evelyn.
This gentleman was one of the most entertaining and
intelligent persons of that age; endowed with extraordinary activity both of mind and body, a "philosopher," as men of science were then called, who was
doing as much as any one in Europe to encourage
research and prepare for the reception of new truth.
He was scarcely less actively interested in the fine
arts and in literature, and he wrote exceedingly well
in English. Evelyn was one of those beings who
dazzle their own generation, and puzzle ours to account
for the fact that they were not absolutely first-rate.
It seems as though nothing but a little more intensity
in any one particular direction was needed to turn
Evelyn from a paragon of all the talents into an
undisputed genius.

This delightful man was in his thirty-fourth year
when Taylor became acquainted with him. Evelyn
had been a gentleman-commoner of Balliol when
Taylor preached his university sermon, but we do not
know that they had met. He had left England when
the Civil War broke out, and he had lived for several
years in Italy, making a very close study of the antiq-
uities and of modern Italian painting, architecture,

and sculpture. He had certainly grown to be the
leading English connoisseur of his time. Then he
had slowly returned northwards, and having married
an English heiress in Paris, he had determined to
venture upon returning to this country, in order to
take up an estate which devolved upon his wife. But
he was unsettled, until, at the opening of 1653, he
obtained possession of the Browne property called
Sayes Court, near Deptford, in Kent, which had
belonged to his wife's family. He was tired of
wandering about the world; he wanted to give
literary form to the innumerable scientific and anti-
quarian notes he had taken, and he began at once,
with feverish eagerness, to lay out the grounds and
furnish the apartments of Sayes Court, that it might
become his retreat.

Evelyn, who at the end of his crowded life was able
truthfully to say that his experience was "all is vanity
which is not honest, and there is no solid wisdom but
in piety," was a devoted Anglican, and was very
desirous of attaching to his household some sequestrated minister of the national church. It was necessary to act with caution, for any public patronage of
clergymen was suspiciously regarded. His choice
originally fell on a worthy divine of Eltham, Richard
Owen, who seems to have acted for a time as private
chaplain at Sayes Court. The active and illuminated
mind of Evelyn, however, with its buoyant ambition,
could hardly receive full satisfaction from the discourses of a humdrum country practitioner. At this
time Cromwell tacitly permitted a single pulpit in
London, that of St. Gregory's, a little church which
stood close to St. Paul's, to be filled by a succession of

Anglican clergy. He doubtless considered that this was a salutary relief for an eloquence which, if pent up too rigorously, might cause a dangerous explosion. On the 15th of March 1654 Evelyn " went to London to hear the famous Dr. Jeremy Taylor at St. Gregory's, concerning evangelical perfection." This was perhaps Evelyn's earliest approach to one who was to take a place among the dearest of his friends.

One of those churchmen with whom Jeremy Taylor was now in frequent correspondence was John Warner, Bishop of Rochester, to whom he dedicated the treatise on Transubstantiation, called *The Real Presence of Christ in the Blessed Sacrament*, which was his solitary publication in 1654. Warner, who was now in his seventieth year, had been one of the most inflexible supporters of Charles I.; in him, as Fuller said, " dying Episcopacy gave the last groan in the House of Lords." He was a most generous benefactor, out of his private purse, to the distressed and ejected clergy; for several years he had been wandering about Wales, doing what kindness he could, and had come into personal contact with Jeremy Taylor, who speaks of the "favours" with which Warner has "already endeared his thankfulness and service," and of the Bishop's having "assisted his condition" out of "the remains" of his "lessened fortunes." The activity and munificence of the ejected Bishop of Rochester were constant thorns in the side of the Parliamentarians, who sequestrated nine-tenths of his large personal estate, and would have imprisoned the indomitable old man if they could only have caught him. Considering that Warner was in the most careful retirement in 1654, it was perhaps more zealous than tactful of Taylor to dedicate a treatise to him by name, although there is nothing in *The Real Presence* fitted to exasperate the political authorities.

In this work Taylor returns to the fight with an old enemy, whom he had long neglected, Rome. He says that the supposed destruction of the Church of England has filled the Romanists with a "strange triumphal gaiety." In particular, he speaks with bitter indignation of one who was formerly the son of the Church of England, "but who ran away from her sorrow, and disinherited himself because she was not able to give him a temporal portion." The utterances of this man, whom Taylor refuses to name, have principally stirred him up to write this book; it is believed that he refers to Bishop Morton's former secretary, John Sarjeaunt, who threw up his post at the beginning of the Civil War, and lived as a priest in a college of seculars at Lisbon until 1652, when he came back to England as a Roman propagandist. Taylor had perhaps had a visit at Golden Grove from Sarjeaunt, for he says that he "has been by chance engaged in a conference with a person of another persuasion," whom in a letter to Sheldon he calls a Jesuit, "the man not unlearned nor unwary."

In *The Real Presence* we are made to feel that Taylor, as a pure man of letters, is slipping away from us. This is a piece of composition seriously inferior to anything else that he had written since he arrived in Wales. It is apparently thrown off in great haste, and Taylor was never at his best when he improvised. It is written to impress those who will be quite indifferent to the charm of his language and the luxuriance of his imagery, and on whom, therefore, he is careful to waste neither of these deliberate ornaments. On the other hand, here, if ever, what was called in theological circles " learning " would be effective, if nowhere else, and Taylor is redundant, from Porphyry and Justin Martyr, in sentences of monstrous prolixity. The arguments of *The Real Presence* were contested, even by those whom they were intended to support, and the author was charged, as of old by Chillingworth in Oxford, with not listening to what his opponents said, and with indulging in illogical rhetoric. The book contains some fine passages, and a few lively ones, but on the whole it is controversy and not literature. It may be noted in passing that Taylor shows himself well acquainted with his Catholic contemporaries in France, and quotes, among others, from the great Arnauld of Port-Royal, as again in later volumes.

Evelyn had evidently introduced himself to Taylor soon after his sitting under him in St. Gregory's. But their intimacy seems to have sprung up in connection with a misfortune which happened to Taylor at the beginning of 1655. It appears that the divine had shown the preface of a new book, *The Golden Grove*, either in manuscript or proof, to Evelyn, who had highly commended its outspoken statement that " never did the excellency of Episcopal government appear so demonstratively and conspicuously as now." That was a hard saying for Parliament and the governing presbyters, who were, moreover, determining upon a more vigorous suppression of Anglican preachers.

In December 1654 the laxity of which the Anglican clergy had been slowly taking advantage was sharply reproved by Parliament. There appeared a general tendency to return to the old intolerant methods, and

the whole question of permitting sectarian worship
was discussed. When Jeremy Taylor went on to
speak of Cromwell as "the son of Zippor," it is no
wonder that Evelyn thought that he was daring the
government to undo him. *The Golden Grove* was
entered at Stationers' Hall on the 26th of January
1655, and exactly a fortnight afterwards Evelyn, who
had been away at Woodcot since New Year's Day,
came home to Sayes Court, and found two letters,
one informing him of Taylor's arrest and the other
of his release. As Evelyn, in consideration of what
The Golden Grove contained, had been very anxious
about his friend's safety, and had been quite prepared
to hear "sad news and deplore your restraint," it is
evident that Taylor's imprisonment was very brief.
Perhaps the proclamation of religious liberty, promulgated on the 15th of February, was the immediate
excuse for his release. We have no light at all upon
the locality where he was confined, but it was probably the Tower of London; he would be required to
pay a fine, and detained until his friends had produced the money.

Deeply sympathising with Taylor's affliction, Evelyn
hastened to strengthen their friendship, and on the 18th
of March went to town on purpose to hear the great
divine preach. Less than a fortnight later Evelyn
had made up his mind to take a serious step, and on
the 31st he "made a visit to Dr. Jeremy Taylor to
confer with him about some spiritual matters, using
him thenceforward as my ghostly father." Many
years afterwards, looking back upon the past, Evelyn
besought God Almighty to keep him thankful for
the impulse which carried him to Taylor, and to make

him always mindful of "his heavenly assistances."
Taylor was manifestly now in danger, but preserved
from it by the zeal and influence of Evelyn, to whom
it was probably due that he was so slow in returning to
his Welsh home. In the meantime the early months
of 1655 present two works for our consideration.

The picturesque title of *The Golden Grove* and its
fiery preface of revolt from under " the harrows and
saws of impertinent and ignorant preachers," are likely
to awaken anticipations in the literary reader which
the body of the treatise can only disappoint. It is a
manual of daily prayers and litanies, so phrased as to
contain a brief summary of all that a Christian should
believe, practise, or desire. It begins with a Short
Catechism, which Taylor hoped would be accepted by
moderate churchmen as a temporary substitute for that
which had been suppressed with the Liturgy. This is
followed by an exposition of the Creed, and that by
" Agenda," or a list of acts of piety to be performed
throughout the day. The next section, " Via Pacis,"
is largely a paraphrase from the *Imitation of Christ*, and
is followed by " Postulanda," a dilution — for we can
call it nothing else — of the Lord's Prayer. Then follow,
concluding the treatise, a set of devotions for the week;
many of these have the purity, and one or two something of the magnificence, of their author, but they are
in his least personal vein. On the whole *The Golden
Grove* offers very little worthy the notice of the literary
student of Taylor's works.

But at the close of it, and appended to it as by an
afterthought, is a slender collection of poems, *Festival
Hymns*, which has the special interest attaching to the
only work in verse which Jeremy Taylor published.

I

He himself indulged in no illusions about the merit of
these exercises. A year later he looked back upon
their publication with a blush, and when Evelyn had
the complaisance to praise them, their author replied,
" I could not but smile at my own weaknesses, and
very much love the great candour and sweetness of
your nature, that you were pleased to endure my
English poetry. But I could not be removed from my
certain knowledge of my own greatest weaknesses in
it." Taylor was also, about this time, translating part
of the *De Rerum Natura* into English verse, but desisted
when he was shown by Evelyn the version of Lucretius
which that philosopher had made. All this is curious
as showing that Jeremy Taylor, about 1655, having
risen to the height of his mastery of prose, was
attempting to extend his sovereignty into the province
of verse. Had he attempted this twenty years earlier,
it is probable that he might have trained himself to be
an accomplished poet of the artificial order; but he made
the experiment too late.

The greater part of the *Festival Hymns* is a sort of
cantata on the mysteries of religion, arranged in connected sections. A quarter of a century had passed
since certain eccentricities of the least happily inspired
pieces in Herbert's *Temple* had opened the door to mere
oddity in the form of religious poetry. The example
of Cowley — although his *Pindarique Odes*, those great
dissolvers of the public taste, were as yet hardly known
— may have had some influence on Taylor. But the
one precedent author whom he had manifestly read,
and whose fantastic innovations in metre he accepted
with alacrity, was Henry Vaughan, the Silurist, the
first part of whose *Silex Scintillans* had appeared in

1650 while the second was dated 1655. It is impossible to connect Vaughan with Taylor in any historical way. But it should be remembered that the lord of Golden Grove was a distant kinsman of the Silurist, that Llandilo and Llansaintffraid were within riding distance of one another, and that in Mrs. Philips, "the Matchless Orinda," of whom we shall presently speak, Henry Vaughan and Jeremy Taylor had an enthusiastic common friend.

The versification in the *Festival Hymns* consists of short lines, arbitrarily broken up by rhymes, and arranged on no rhythmical principle. No system could be less tuneful, and in comparison with these hymns the worst odes of Cowley and even of Flatman are musical; what is curious in so learned a writer, Taylor's rhymes are often scarcely assonances. It was certainly in the *Silex Scintillans* that Taylor found his model for his eccentricity of metre; we may perhaps go further, and in Vaughan's irregular canticles called "The Jews" and "Jesus Weeping" detect the identical poems which Taylor read at the close of 1654 and straightway sat down to imitate. He was far too skilful a craftsman to fail to produce something ingenious, and the following passage may be quoted as presenting Jeremy Taylor at his best as a poet: —

> " What ravish'd heart, seraphic tongue or eyes,
> 　　　Clear as the morning's rise,
> 　　　Can speak, or think, or see
> 　　　That bright eternity ?
> 　There the King's great transparent throne
> 　　Is of an éntire jasper stone :
> 　　　There the eye
> 　　　Of the chrysolite,
> 　　　And a sky

Of diamonds, rubies, chrysoprase,
  And above all, Thy holy face,
  Makes an eternal clarity.
When Thou Thy jewels up dost bind, that day
  Remember us, we pray."

It would be difficult to find a more instructive text
on which to expatiate upon the essential difference
between poetry and prose. For here are all the elements of imagination and of language which Taylor
would have employed in building up one of his dazzling
prose sentences, lifting it into our vision like some
perfect marble campanile against the blue Italian sky.
But this strophe is a mere mistake; it has neither the
plastic harmony of prose, nor the severer and more
mechanical beauty of verse. It misses either perfection, and is merely a brilliant instance of the failure
of a great genius to express itself in an unfamiliar
medium.

On the 3rd of May 1655 Jeremy Taylor's unlucky
volume, the *Unum Necessarium*, the production of which,
though he acted in the purest good faith, was to destroy
his peace of mind and make him an army of enemies,
was entered at Stationers' Hall. It was not published,
however, until October, and we now enter a very
troubled and painful period of Taylor's life, where the
sequence of causes and events is extremely obscure.
What seems to be certain is that, having corrected the
proofs of his book, he left for Wales in May, and on
the road was arrested and thrown into Chepstow Castle.
What was the reason of this second imprisonment?
It has been attributed to the sentiments of the *Unum
Necessarium*, but the tenor of that work offered no excuse
for such persecution had it been known, and, as we now

find, it was not yet published. If the divine had been arrested for unlawful preaching in London, it would not have been in Chepstow but in the Tower that we should have found him. And the harsh treatment which he received from old church friends, like Duppa and Warner, would have been peculiarly untimely and unkind. The correspondence with these people, and with others, during Taylor's captivity, offers no sort of suggestion that he was confined for conscience' sake. The present writer has unwillingly come to the conclusion that Taylor was probably arrested at the suit of some Welsh creditor, and for a debt which he could not pay.

Taylor's poverty at this period of his life was extreme. Bishop Heber thought that he was married by this time to Joanna Bridges, and through this second wife possessed " a competent estate." But a careful examination of the correspondence shows this to be a mistake. Taylor's letters of this time are pitiful in their confession of poverty, and for reasons which are not beyond conjecture neither Evelyn on the one hand nor Carbery on the other seemed to be willing to advance him money. The *Unum Necessarium* has a dedication to Lord Carbery, which is dragged in very awkwardly, because the book had already, and much more appropriately, been introduced by a letter to Duppa and Warner. Perhaps, as his distresses gathered about him, he rapidly wrote the dedication to Lord Carbery as an appeal to his generosity; and in that case he was disappointed, for Lord Carbery evidently did not respond. And now, quite abruptly, Lord Carbery's name disappears from the chronicle of Taylor's life. When he was released from Chepstow, it was not

to Llanfihangel-Aberbythych that he proceeded, but
to the house of Joanna Bridges, at Man-dinam. Nor,
in spite of all that his biographers have said, is there
any evidence that Taylor ever visited Golden Grove
again.

Jeremy Taylor had lived too long in the shelter of
an irresponsible asylum to face the world, and such a
rough world, with any discretion. Everything which
he did, on the occasion of his venturing from his Welsh
retreat, was lacking in ripeness of judgment. The year
1655 is marked at every turn by the amiable and
enthusiastic divine's defect of common sense. In the
first place, it was most rash and unworldly to advertise
his retreat publicly and needlessly by calling his
catechism for the use of anti-Parliamentarian persons,
with its reckless preface, *The Golden Grove*. It is reasonable to infer that when he was thrown into prison,
on the first occasion, for the outspoken opposition of
this work to the ruling of the House of Commons,
Cromwell's attention was drawn to the title, and that
Lord Carbery was sharply called to order for the in-
discretions of his chaplain. Moreover, it had been
announced that after November 1 it would be illegal
for him to keep a chaplain in his house at all, on pain
of banishment and sequestration. The position of the
ejected clergy had therefore become one of great peril
to their friends, though, as it proved, the practice of
the law was less vindictive than its theory. But Lord
Carbery was a timid man, and nothing we know of his
character would lead us to suppose that he would
hesitate for one moment in sacrificing his clerical friend
to the safety of his estates. If this be the case, it
accounts for the sudden cessation of all reference to

Golden Grove, and for Taylor's unpleasant surprise when, poor already, he approached his home, to find himself deprived of the only means of support left to him.

At such a moment, a man more worldly-wise would have acted with discretion, but Taylor had nothing of the serpent in his disposition. For some reason, which it is impossible to determine, Evelyn thought it proper, or wise, or perhaps really kind, to allow him to remain in Chepstow Castle for the present, merely looking about to provide a means of living for him when once he was released. In this conjuncture, Taylor had no influential friends but the High Church associates of his old Oxford days, several of whom were wealthy, and all had been well-disposed to him. But precisely in May 1655, as we shall now find, he had contrived to offend every one of them.

In March, soon after his original release, Taylor had had an interview with the Bishop of Salisbury, Brian Duppa, who was up in London on one of his rare visits. Two or three years earlier Taylor had consulted Duppa, the one living churchman whose opinion he always seems most eager to conciliate, about "the body of cases of conscience" which he had so long had on his mind, and which eventually, after a thousand vicissitudes, saw the light as that most elephantine of all theological works, the *Ductor Dubitantium*. In the preparation of this book Jeremy Taylor displayed an extraordinary firmness, which it is perhaps not derogatory to his virtue to call an amazing obstinacy. Nobody welcomed the *Ductor Dubitantium*. The publisher, eager to receive whatever else came from Taylor's pen, rejected or postponed it time after time.

Duppa, indeed, not only "assented" to the scheme of it,
when it was first laid before him, but "desired Taylor
to proceed seriously and soberly with it," and promised
"to pray for a blessing on the undertaking." But
when Duppa said that, he had not seen the work.

Driven inexorably by his conscience, and caring
nothing for what the temporal results might be,
Taylor pushed forward the vast scheme, but the more
his friends saw of it the less they liked it. Meanwhile, Taylor became aware that it was "necessary by
way of introduction [to a monograph on the conscience]
to premit in a more general way the doctrine and
practice of repentance." He laid this scheme also
before Duppa, and the Bishop of Salisbury, though
obviously a little anxious, gave a prudent sanction
to this, although he suspected that on the subject of
a late repentance Jeremy Taylor held unusual views.
But while Duppa warned him, "with a fatherly confidence," that in the very difficult matter he had
undertaken he would "need a prudence more than
ordinary," the Bishop did not so much as dream that
Taylor would leap into a still more terrible thorn-
bush, and advance what seemed to be positive heresy
on the dogma of original sin. In the face of all this,
it was indeed a saintly simplicity which led Taylor
to inscribe the book on repentance, which neither
prelate had seen, to Brian Duppa, as Bishop of Salisbury, and to John Warner, as Bishop of Rochester.
Meanwhile, Chepstow Castle opened its jaws and
swallowed up the hapless Taylor.

But Royston, who had secured the manuscript,
alarmed by the catastrophe, stopped the printing for
some months, and it was not until August that he

bethought him of sending to Duppa a portion of the book. He forwarded a bundle of proofs, without beginning or end, and without any indication whether it was by Taylor's wish or not that he sent them. Duppa read what was consigned to him, first with bewilderment, then with horror, then with angry indignation. Here was a book, the publication of which Duppa had no power to stop, which might be supposed to have received the approbation of the Bishop of Rochester and himself, a book which attacked, in his judgment and Warner's, that "integrity," that is to say that orthodoxy, which was dearer to them both than their own lives. And here was the author of that book absolutely unapproachable, in prison; while the least publicity would only increase the scandal which the sequestrated bishops feared so much.

At all events, if Jeremy Taylor could not be approached, he could be written to. Duppa, though the mildest and kindest of men, was roused to vehement anger. He wrote to the imprisoned Taylor, and told him in the sharpest terms "what a scandal it would bring upon his poor desolate mother, the Church, which is likely to receive a greater wound by this unwary blow of his than by all the unreasonable acts of persecution which her malicious enemies have done against her." Duppa wrote a great deal more of this kind, and even "could not forbear to write sharper things than these." Jeremy Taylor replied, gently and regretfully, but "it seems," as Duppa complained to his friends, "that nothing could work upon him." Taylor wrote to defend his views, not to excuse them. When Duppa wrote again, Taylor did not answer.

The bishops comforted themselves that perhaps the book would never appear, and that if it did, no one would know that they had seemed to encourage it in its inception. Meanwhile, Royston, having plucked up heart, proceeded with the printing, and in October the *Unum Necessarium* was published in London. What was the horror of Duppa and Warner to find, when they turned to it, that the terrible and embarrassing volume was dedicated to them both. All our love for Jeremy Taylor cannot prevent our sympathising with the Bishop of Salisbury in his scream of indignation. "Without any way of acquainting me with it, he has been pleased to make use of my name in the very forehead of it!"

It was part of Taylor's unworldly simplicity that he could not be made to see that he ought not to have done this. He had written a very severe treatise on a difficult theological point, which he desired to bring strenuously under the notice of the Bishops of Salisbury and Rochester. He did not for a moment realise that by dedicating the work to them he pledged them to a support of his views. In his lack of business experience, he did not perceive the extremely delicate position in which he was placing the ex-prelates, nor the injury he was doing them in identifying them with doctrines which were detestable to them. Warner seems to have taken the matter philosophically, but Duppa was excessively agitated, and actually sent round privately, among his friends, a sort of circular denouncing Taylor's arguments. He says, "If I by my silence should have given way to them, I should have been highly guilty, and deservedly lost myself in the opinion of all good men." The stir produced among churchmen by the *Unum Necessarium* justified, it must be admitted, Duppa's nervous apprehensions.

The book has long ceased to awaken alarm, and its principal fault may now seem to be a wearisome prolixity, a hammering at nails which were already up to their heads in every instructed conscience. Probably, but for one chapter, the nature of which has already been briefly mentioned, even seventeenth-century readers would not have been scandalised by it. The *Unum Necessarium* is a treatise written with the purpose " that the strictnesses of a holy life be thought necessary, and that repentance may be no more that trifling little piece of duty to which the errors of the late schools of learning, and the desires of men to be deceived in this article, have reduced it." This was a subject fit for a single sermon, but it scarcely needed such very lengthy treatment in so thick a volume. But the importance of repentance had been interesting Taylor more and more; it was " a *catholicon* to the evils of the soul of every man." The book is, in fact, a chip, or rather a log, from the workshop of his immense *Ductor Dubitantium*. His investigations into the psychology of conscience led him to insist on the necessity of a holy life. He found people willing to go on living in a condition of sin without danger or reproof, hoping all would be well at the last. This state of mind was a stumbling-block to Jeremy Taylor, who argued, properly enough, that if a holy life is not necessary, it is mere waste of time for a theologian to go into a vast series of nice cases of conscience. But what are men bound to repent of ? This question led him into the very thorny province of original sin, where unfortunately he was the victim of what one of his

warmest admirers has called "an inaccuracy of reasoning which led him into a partial heterodoxy." The
heresy consisted in a denial "that the depravation of
man's nature after the fall was so total as had been
generally apprehended." This conviction led Taylor
to hold that repentance is not applicable to original
sin, because a man cannot be asked to repent of a state
of things entirely beyond his own control.

It was the chapter on original sin, and not the
treatment of death-bed repentances, which caused
the scandal. In fact, as regards the second of these
dogmas, the author slightly reduces the severity which
he had shown in earlier books, and here he was supported by a capable champion in Hammond. But his
treatment of the former found no friends, and Taylor
continued to languish under a suspicion of Pelagian
error which affected all the rest of his career. The
private correspondence of the time, even more than
the published attacks, proves the dismay with which
the chapter on original sin was received. An appeal
was made to the venerable Sanderson, as the most dignified churchman of the age, to refute it; but, as a curious
letter, now in the Bodleian, from Sanderson to Barlow
shows, without avail. Sanderson shrewdly considered
that "in these times of so much distraction, as little
notice should be taken of differences amongst ourselves
as is possible." Moreover, Taylor, who usually forwarded presentation copies of his works to Sanderson
as soon as they appeared, had been careful not to
send the *Unum Necessarium* to that Bishop, who, as
late as September 25, 1656, had not so much as seen it.
Others were not so discreet as Sanderson. Dr. Peter
Samwayes, writing apparently to Sancroft, declares

in an unpublished letter that he "values not what Dr. Taylor says unless it be according to the Scriptures and the doctrine of the Church," and urges a general repudiation of his errors. Warner was dreadfully distressed, and declared that "Pelagius had puddled the stream" of Taylor's faith. The amiable and indulgent Sheldon expostulated with Taylor for his "folly and frowardness." Never was such a consensus of reprobation. But Taylor remained quite calm under the storm, and theological opinion nowadays will record, without the least horror, that, in his opinion, though not, perhaps, in his arguments, he was, as usual, far ahead of his age in liberality.

He occupied the close of his imprisonment at Chepstow Castle in replying to the objections of his critics in a little volume, called *Deus Justificatus*, in which he stood to his guns, and charged the Anglican divines with having borrowed their gloss from the Presbyterians. This reply took the form of a letter to Christiana, Dowager Countess of Devonshire, who appears to have befriended him in prison, and who perhaps sent him, with a gift of money, a request for a further explanation of his theory. This lady was equally interested in poetry and in theology. She kept open house for the royalist wits at Roehampton, and had been celebrated in verse by Donne in her girlhood, and by Waller in her middle life. It is not certain in what manner the *Deus Justificatus* reached the public. Royston published it in 1656, not only without the author's consent, but apparently without Lady Devonshire's knowledge. In a letter, Royston says that Taylor was very angry with him, and the publisher grovelled with excuses, for Taylor was perhaps the most valuable author on his list. We may doubt whether Taylor was really displeased at this publication, or at that of his correspondence on the same subject with Bishop Warner.

In writing from Chepstow Castle in September 1656 Taylor says that "the gentlemen under whose custody I am, as they are careful of their charges, so are they civil to my person." At first they seem to have prevented him from receiving letters, but this embargo was presently removed. On the 5th of November Sheldon forgave him in a kind letter, in which he relieved him of an old debt, and apparently lent him a further sum which enabled him to regain his freedom. A few days later Taylor has left his prison, but he retires, not to Golden Grove, which was to see him no more, but to Man-dinam, whither, apparently, his children had already found an asylum with Joanna Bridges. Of this lady little is known, and a mystery hangs over her birth. The egregious Lady Wray pretended to believe that Joanna was a natural child of King Charles I.; the estate of Man-dinam was certainly her personal property. Whether Taylor was already married to her is quite unknown, but his extreme poverty in the winter of 1655–56 seems to preclude the idea. She was probably at this time merely his benefactress, whose hospitality was extended to him as a celebrated and afflicted clergyman, to whom any royalist lady of means would be happy to offer a home. Man-dinam, which was her property, was, and still is, a small country-house on an estate two miles east of the village of Llangadock. It is romantically situated on a hill above the south side of the Brân River, just where that stream narrows its gorge before spreading into the Vale of Towey; it commands a fine view south to the Rhiwiau Hills and the Black Mountain. Man-dinam is ten or twelve miles from Golden Grove, by the road which passes through Llandilo and Llangadock; it remained the property of Joanna Bridges after she became Mrs. Taylor, and until her death.

Lord Carbery had by this time married again. His new wife was Lady Alice Egerton, daughter of the first Earl of Bridgewater, who had died in 1649. It was she who, as a child, had taken parts in the *Comus* and in the *Arcades* of Milton, and to whom, on account of her known interest in the art of music, Lawes dedicated his *Airs and Dialogues* in 1653. There is evidence that Jeremy Taylor tried to propitiate her, in rather a clumsy way; for, when printing a third edition of *The Great Exemplar*, he cancelled the dedication of the third book, which he had inscribed to the first countess, his dear friend, and inserted a letter of compliment in its place to the stranger. There is no evidence that Alice, Lady Carbery, took any interest in Taylor, or extended any species of patronage to him, and perhaps she was not pleased at the divine's reminder that she came to Golden Grove as the " successor to a very dear and most excellent person."

Evelyn, who, as has been said, seems to have had some good reason for being unwilling to help his friend as long as he was in Chepstow Castle, now hastened to offer counsel and aid. He advised Taylor to come at once to town, but the reply (on the 5th of January 1656) was, " Sir, I know not when I shall be able to come to London, for our being stripped of the little relics of our fortune remaining after the shipwreck leaves not cordage

or sails sufficient to bear me thither." He was in sorry
plight, indeed, for some one now "blew the coals," and
stirred up fresh resentment in his only friend among
the bishops, Sheldon. In spite of his wretched poverty,
however, and the pressure from all sides, Taylor per-
sisted in refusing to recant his views, or explain them
away. But Evelyn had now interested in the case
Mr. Thurland (afterwards Sir Edward and a baron of
the Exchequer), who was a prominent royalist lawyer,
and a zealous supporter of the church. A proposition
was made that Taylor should undertake some work of
propaganda, and on the 19th of January he is expecting
suddenly to go into Nottinghamshire for a fortnight.
As he had no money of his own, this must have been
a professional journey paid for by a client, in all probability Thurland, whose country-house was Gamelton
Hall, in Nottinghamshire. Nothing seems to have been
arranged at once, and it was a very dangerous time,
for there was a recrudescence of persecution, and
Cromwell was showing renewed severity to the clergy.
Two months later Evelyn is alarmed with "apprehensions" of Taylor's "danger," an alarm which presently
subsides under some report of a fortunate nature.
But "the daily sacrifice is ceasing, and the exercise of
[sacerdotal] functions is made criminal, and the light
of Israel is quenched." But "Julianus Redivivus can
shut the schools, indeed, and the temples, but he cannot
hinder our private intercourses and devotions, where
the breast is the chapel and our heart is the altar."
Then follows a little period of repose, when the eye
of the accuser seems to be removed from our divine,
and we find him enjoying easy social intercourse with
the excellent Evelyn and his friends.

Evelyn carried his confessor off to Sayes Court, where on the 12th of April the house-party comprised, besides Taylor, two of the most eminent living men of science, Robert Boyle, the natural philosopher, and John Wilkins, Warden of Wadham, who was just about to marry Cromwell's sister Robinia. The acquaintance of Wilkins, who, although on the popular side, was anxious to propitiate the distressed clergy and to lighten their burdens, must have been particularly valuable to Taylor at this juncture. Wilkins and Evelyn were now extremely intimate, while the new relation of the latter with Taylor was increasing Evelyn's zeal for the Anglican form of religion.

It is now necessary to examine a bibliographical *crux* which has greatly puzzled Jeremy Taylor's biographers, and is of some vital importance. If we were to decide that the *Auxiliary Beauty* is a genuine work of Taylor, we should be obliged to modify our estimate of his character in some curious particulars. In the course of the agitated year 1656 Royston published a small anonymous volume, entitled *A Discourse of Auxiliary Beauty, or Artificial Handsomeness. In Point of Conscience between Two Ladies.* This is in fact a treatise in defence of the use of cosmetics, in the form of a dialogue between two persons of quality, the one an austerely Puritanic lady, "a severe censurer of all extern helps to beauty," the other an orthodox churchwoman, of a more modern type, who claims the right, as a Christian woman, of repairing by the use of rouge and similar appliances the ravages of her complexion. The Puritan makes a very feeble resistance, and, although she produces "a black and ponderous cloud of witnesses," she is borne down by

K

the tide of arguments and instances poured forth by
her opponent. The line of defence is briefly this, that
no one objects to the restoration of the teeth or even
the hair by artificial means; for instance, we may
"use, if we list, a crystal, painted eye," and give no
offence to the most precise. The cosmeticist asks, in
triumph, " When was your ladyship scandalised with
any grave and sober matron because she laid out the
combings or cuttings of her own hair or others' more
youthful hair, when her own, now more withered and
autumnal, seemed less becoming to her ? " Why, then,
be so pedantic as to object to a touch of ceruse on the
faded cheek ?

Quite early there arose a legend that Jeremy Taylor
was connected with this somewhat ingenious piece of
special pleading. It was brought out by Taylor's
publisher, and in 1662 a second edition of it appeared
with the initials " J. T., D.D." on the title-page, initials
which Taylor himself had used in publishing his own
avowed secular production, the *Discourse of Friendship*.
This was five years before his death, and we have no
evidence that he took any steps to deny the impeach-
ment; it is true that he had left London at the time,
and was in Ireland. In the third edition the attribu-
tion to " a late learned bishop " was more explicit still,
and the work continues to figure in our bibliographical
catalogues of Taylor's works. Meanwhile Anthony à
Wood had included the *Auxiliary Beauty* in a list of
the writings of Jeremy Taylor, while, finally, White
Kennett, Bishop of Peterborough, also attributed it to
him. This evidence of Kennett's merely shows that
after the Restoration it was general subject of gossip
that Taylor had composed this discourse. Such is the

external evidence, and if it collected around a work which was in harmony with Taylor's character and bore evidence of his style, it must be confessed that it could hardly be resisted.

But in this case internal evidence is overwhelming in the other scale of the balance. In the first instance, if we turn to the treatise itself we find the publisher making a definite statement. The MS. was brought to him, he says, anonymously; but, "of this discourse, as I am certainly informed, a woman was not only the chief occasion, but the author and writer." Everything in the body of the tract supports this view. It is an example of the kind of picturesque, audacious writing which women were, at that moment in the history of our literature, beginning to introduce, and of which there had already been several striking examples. There is a certain amount of theology in it, especially towards the end, where two Puritan books of the reign of James I., Downham's *Christian Warfare* and Perkins's *Cases of Conscience*, are carefully controverted so far as they forbid the use of cosmetics. Some of Taylor's pet phrases are introduced, not, however, as he would use them himself, but as a lady who had attended his ministrations might be expected to repeat them. Taylor may be referred to as " a witty and eloquent preacher whom we both heard at Oxford." Examples of what may be called the pseudo-Taylorian manner may easily be found; for instance, the Cosmetic Lady speaks of "persons who sometimes appear pallidly sad, as if they were going to their graves, otherwhiles with such a rosy cheerfulness, as if they had begun their resurrection." This is a conscious or unconscious parody of Taylor's style, but no one who is accustomed to his phrases will mistake it for the genuine thing. Even more hopelessly unlike is the attitude of the writer, her pious levity, her lack of all real spirituality, her superficial unction in making the best of both worlds. Finally, all the external evidence which could be produced would fail to persuade us that Jeremy Taylor wrote, especially in the sad and troubled year 1656, pert sentences of which the following is a very fair example, where the author, after saying that the clergy had objected to tobacco, remarks that now they have generally taken it to themselves, "fancying at last that they never had more devout meditations or sharp inventions than those begotten by a pipe of good tobacco, which now perfumes their clothes, their books, their studies, and their sermons"; and this, not in reproof, but in sheer levity.

It would be pitiful to take this satyr for our Hyperion, yet there persists in the mind a feeling that Taylor must have been in some way concerned with the *Auxiliary Beauty* for so strenuous a legend to connect him with it. There is every likelihood that the title is his. In my own mind the probable issue is that Taylor was intrusted with the MS., perhaps against his will, by some great lady in the orthodox camp, whose request that he would submit it to Royston it was impossible for him to refuse. Such a lady might very probably be Christiana, Countess of Devonshire, a blue-stocking, an ardent churchwoman, a relic of the old Oxford days, and a frequenter of the worldly wits. She was an admirer of Taylor, she had lately made him a debtor by her benevolence, and for all her formal piety, she was nothing of a precisian.

If we suppose Lady Devonshire making the request, it is difficult to see how Taylor could possibly decline to submit her MS. to Royston, and if she went further and asked him to read it and even to revise, he would find in it nothing to which he could take any direct objection. The present writer must, however, endorse Heber's opinion, and say that he little cares who may have written the *Auxiliary Beauty*, " provided it does not pass for Taylor's." The difficulty, however, still remains that Taylor did not deny the authorship in his lifetime.

The exact business which attracted Taylor to London in the early months of 1656 is nowhere precisely stated, but it was connected with Mr. Thurland, and it was of a confidentially ecclesiastical character. The jealousy of the government and the watchful zeal of Cromwell's myrmidons well account for the secrecy which was preserved. But Taylor was evidently engaged in some agency which aimed at keeping up communication between the ejected bishops and their clergy. On the 6th of May Evelyn brought a young French Sorbonnist, M. Le Franc, who was an Anglican convert, " to converse with Dr. Taylor," who was much pleased with him, and recommended him to a divine whom Evelyn calls " the Bishop of Meath." This is a slip of the pen, for the deprived Bishop of Meath had long been dead, and none other, of course, could be appointed to the vacant see, until the Restoration. Whoever the prelate was, he was " very poor and in great want," and only too glad to get the fees, which Evelyn paid, with the exclamation, " To that necessity are our clergy reduced!" In July Mr. Thurland's " kindnesses " make it possible that Taylor will be able to settle in or near London, which he would do at once, if only he were not "hindered by my *res angusta domi.*" He is waiting to see the *Deus Justificatus* published, and then hopes to come to a definite understanding with Mr. Thurland.

We have heard nothing of Jeremy Taylor's family since the death of his wife in 1651. It appears that his mother in-law, Mrs. Langsdale, formed part of his household at Golden Grove, having doubtless come to take charge of his motherless children. A letter dated November 24, 1653, written to his brother-in-law, "at his apothecary's house in Gainsborough," exemplifies the writer's tenderness. Edward Langsdale has been dangerously ill, but Taylor had not had the heart to alarm his mother, until news came of the patient's recovery, when she could be "troubled and pleased at the same time." He was a kind and solicitous parent, cultivating towards his children "sweetness of conversation, affability, frequent admonitions, all significations of love and tenderness, care and watchfulness." After they had lost their mother, he redoubled his solicitude, and was more than ever "pitiful and gentle, complying with all their infirmities." But now, just at the moment when he was broken in fortune and uprooted from his resting-place, he was to be most cruelly afflicted in his tenderest feelings. Early in July 1656 a little son died, — "A boy," says his father in writing to Evelyn, "that lately made us very glad, but now he rejoices in his little orb, while we think and sigh and long to be as safe as he is." But there was worse in store for him.

Early in 1657 there broke out an epidemic of small-pox at Man-dinam, and "two sweet hopeful boys" of

Jeremy Taylor's were among the victims. He had now, of five sons, but one surviving, Charles, who was to die a few days before his father in 1667. The sons who died in 1657 have been spoken of as "young men," but the elder of them could not have been more than fourteen years of age. The blow to their father was overwhelming; "I shall tell you," he writes to Evelyn, "that I have passed through a great cloud which hath wetted me deeper than the skin." His sorrow was so bitter that it rendered him "an object of every good man's pity and commiseration." He could think of nothing else, and had to beg pardon of Thurland for neglecting his business and failing to reply to his letters. At length, about Easter, he shook off his depression, and determined to leave Wales for good. Rust says that the loss of his sons so sensibly affected his spirits, that he could no longer endure to live in the place where they had been. He came up to London and settled in secret, doubtless under Thurland's protection. Jeremy Taylor now withdraws for a while beneath a dense cloud, through which we perceive no more light than is given us by the statement that "he officiated in a private congregation of loyalists, to his great hazard and danger." As the year proceeded, the difficulties in the way of Anglican public worship became insurmountable. In August Evelyn notes that for the first time the Church has been "reduced to a chamber and a conventicle, so sharp is the persecution," and zealous Christians met in private houses. Even then they were liable to be disturbed by sudden raids of soldiers, who dispersed the worshippers with their muskets. In this sorrowful condition the godly were thrust back upon contempla-

tion and reverie, and from the suffering Church of
England there arose a murmur of resignation, and a
song of —

> " O crux ave spes unica
>   Hoc passionis tempore :
>   Auge piis justitiam,
>   Reisque dona veniam."

Taylor's patience had sustained the burden of all the
attacks which had been made upon it, when it suddenly
gave way beneath a straw.   A certain bitter Puritan
divine, Henry Jeanes by name, was rector of Chedzoy
in Somerset.   He was a provocative disputant, dab-
bling much in printers' ink, and "pecking and hewing
continually at logic and physics."   On a summer's day,
a friend of his came out from Bridgwater to visit
Jeanes; this gentleman, Mr. T. C., was a very ardent
admirer of Jeremy Taylor.   He sang his praises so
loudly that Jeanes, who had begun by assenting, and
by acknowledging Taylor's "admirable wit, great
parts, quick and elegant pen, abilities in critical learning, and profound skill in antiquity," felt obliged to
remark what a pity it was that Taylor held erroneous
ideas on various points, and particularly on the subject of original sin.   A copy of the *Deus Justificatus*
happened to lie on the window-sill of the rectory at
Chedzoy, and the friends began to turn over its pages.
When Jeanes, thoroughly exasperated, had called the
book a mass of gross nonsense and blasphemy, T. C.
became scandalised, refused to argue any more, and
announced that he should lay Jeanes's objections before
Jeremy Taylor himself.   Jeanes agreed, but insisted
on writing out those objections in a letter; which was
duly forwarded.   To this Taylor made a stubborn

reply, and Jeanes, now quite in his element, flung
himself into the fray. Taylor was full of troubles and
anxieties at the time, and, as he wrote to the Matchless
Orinda, " so pushed at by herds and flocks of people
that follow anybody that whistles to them, or drives
them to pasture, that I am grown afraid of any truth
that seems chargeable with singularity." His replies
to Jeanes's attacks show his irritability by their
violence and roughness. Jeanes, who was engaged in
fighting Hammond in 1657, did not print the correspondence with Taylor until 1660, when he brought it
out in a little quarto, and also published a volume
called *Original Righteousness*, which was a venomous
diatribe against Taylor. It is to be feared that, in
delaying the publication of his attacks until the
Restoration, Jeanes was acting maliciously. Taylor
took no further notice of him.

In May of this year a plan which Evelyn had long
entertained of a subscription for the support of Jeremy
Taylor seems to have been carried out. Several
wealthy royalists, " sensible of this opportunity to do
God and their country an acceptable service," guaran-
teed an annual salary, in return for which he was to
preach in private houses, administer the communion,
and perform other priestly offices confidentially, without attracting the notice of the authorities. An extremely grateful and loving letter from Taylor (May
15) testifies to the relief which this arrangement
gave to his anxious care. His whole prospect, which
had been very dark for the past three years, now
sensibly brightened, and we see the effect in the gay
and graceful composition which proceeded next from
his pen. In the month of June he finished and sent

to press his beautiful *Discourse of Friendship*, which
appeared before the summer of 1657 reached its close.
All through this year the references to Evelyn are
numerous, and we find Taylor frequently going down
to Sayes Court for a burial or a christening, to confirm
the faith of the residents, or simply to be himself
refreshed by his host's liberal and graceful hospitality.

At what date Jeremy Taylor formed the acquaintance of Orinda is uncertain. That eminent lady, whose
real name was Mrs. Katherine Philips, had come to
South Wales in 1647, in her seventeenth year, as the
wife of a royalist gentleman, the owner of Cardigan
Priory. One of her pieces is a greeting to the third
Countess of Carbery on her marriage; but with this
exception her curious and tantalising collection of very
personal poems does not connect her with the little
group of friends at Golden Grove. Mrs. Philips is
supposed to have adopted the name of Orinda in 1651,
when she began to collect around her at Cardigan a
Society of Friendship, to which men were admitted,
but which mainly consisted of women. Orinda was
not pretty, but she was extremely animated, witty,
and agreeable. She became, in those dark days, very
easily the unquestioned Muse and Sibyl of South
Wales. She dubbed the members of her society by
romantic names, such as Rosania, Polycrite, Poliarchus,
and Regina. Under these pseudonyms she addressed
her friends, but particularly the ladies, in terms of
burning enthusiasm. Sometimes she inadvertently
gave the same name to two persons in succession, as
when she called a Mr. Francis Finch "the excellent
Palæmon," and then transferred the title, as "the noble
Palæmon," to Jeremy Taylor, with this result, that a

long poem which she addressed either to the one or to the other "on his incomparable *Discourse of Friendship*" has been supposed to belong to Finch, although there is no reason to believe that he ever wrote anything of the kind.

Although she lived buried in the country, was only twenty-six years of age, and had published nothing, Orinda was already celebrated. She was introducing a new sort of sentimentality, an effusive celebration of friendship between persons of the same sex, which was quite fresh in England, and which attracted a great deal of attention. Her verses, which lack colour and music, but are not without intellectual strength, were passed eagerly from hand to hand. Orinda took very high ground; she proposed something novel in philosophy and in morals, and she wished to link her newly discovered virtue with piety. In one of her odes to the most adored of her companions, Miss Anne Owen of Landshipping, she had exclaimed —

> " Come, my Lucasia, since we see
>   That miracles man's faith do move,
> By wonder and by prodigy
>   To the dull, angry world let 's prove
>   There 's a religion in our love."

Perhaps the dull, angry world of Cardigan had challenged this assertion, for Orinda laid before Jeremy Taylor the inquiry: " How far is a dear and perfect friendship authorised by the principles of Christianity ? " His reply grew into what is one of the most beautiful of his minor writings, *A Discourse of the Nature and Offices of Friendship*, which appeared in 1657, with a dedication to " the most ingenious and excellent Mrs. Katharine Philips."

After a splendid compliment to the lady, already
" so eminent in friendships," Taylor begins to examine
the theme in his customary lucid way, but with more
melody and amenity than he had shown in his writings
for several years past.   He is less strenuous in this
social matter than he is accustomed to be in matters of
theology.   He admits that the New Testament does
not recognise friendship as a Christian virtue, in
Orinda's sense, but deals with charity to mankind,
which is of universal warrant.   Yet the whole may
include the part, and as our graces here below are all
imperfect, we must make the best we can of those
partial and fragmentary instincts which drive us to
cultivate the affections of certain persons whom we
isolate from the mass of those who claim our universal
charity.   In theory friendship should embrace all the
inhabitants of the globe; but our hearts are finite, and
in practice our love is limited.

" Some have only a dark day and a long night from [the
sun], snows and white cattle, a miserable life, and a perpetual
harvest of catarrhs and consumptions, apoplexies and dead
palsies.   But some have splendid fires and aromatic spices,
rich wines and well-digested fruits, great wit and great courage,
because they dwell in his eye, and look in his face, and are
the courtiers of the sun, and wait upon him in his chambers
of the east.   Just so it is in friendships.   Some are worthy,
and some are necessary.   Some dwell hard by and are fitted
for converse.   Nature joins some to us, and religion combines
us with others.   Society and accidents, parity of fortune and
equal dispositions do actuate our friendships ; which, of themselves and in their prime disposition, are prepared for all mankind according as any one can receive them."

From this Taylor proceeds to indicate how strong
and how legitimate a part must be taken by instinctive

attraction in the approach to one another of those
who are about to become friends. Many qualities
enter into the alchemy of this enchanting state, which
is "nothing but love and society mixed together." He
dwells on the innocency of it, the subtlety, the refreshment and cordial which it gives to the soul, and he
bids those who are mutually attracted not to resist
the magnetism, but to fly to one another, to enjoy the
transports of sympathy and happiness, only being
careful not to be so infatuated as to be unable to pass
judgment on the moral worth of the proposed friend.
Charm of conversation, unity of interests, wit, physical beauty and harmony of thought, all these he
admits as natural and proper forces leading to the
mystery of friendship, but there should be close care
taken, before the two souls are blinded by intimacy,
that none of these is at work alone, but that the soul
of him towards which our soul leans forward is pure
and honest. He will not make a man his *privado*, his
special and peculiar friend, unless he be a good as
well as an attractive one.

"I choose this man" he says "to be my friend, because he
is able to give me counsel, to restrain my wanderings, to comfort me in my sorrows. He is pleasant to me in private and
useful in public. He will make my joys double, and divide my
grief between himself and me. For what else should I choose
him? For being a fool and useless? For a pretty face and
a smooth chin? I confess it is possible to be a friend to one
who is ignorant and pitiable, handsome and good-for-nothing,
that eats well and drinks deep. But he cannot be a friend to
me, and I love him with a fondness or a pity, but it cannot be
a noble friendship."

When once he is launched on a disquisition of what
friendship is, and what it means in a man's private

life, as a source of comfort and refreshment, his eloquence knows no bounds; he proceeds in a kind of
golden rapture, the fancies clustering round him and
delaying the progress of his argument. Nowhere is
he more dithyrambic: —

"I will love a worthy friend that can delight me as well as
profit me, rather than him who cannot delight me at all, and
profit me no more. Yet I will not weigh the gayest flowers,
or the wings of butterflies, against wheat; but when I am to
choose wheat, I may take that which looks the brightest. I
had rather see thyme and roses, marjoram and July flowers,
that are fair and sweet and medicinal, than the prettiest tulips
that are good for nothing. My sheep and kie are better servants than race-horses and greyhounds, and I shall rather
furnish my study with Plutarch and Cicero, with Livy and
Polybius, than with *Cassandra* and *Ibrahim Bassa*. If I do
give an hour to these for divertisement or pleasure, yet I will
dwell with them that can instruct me, and make me wise and
eloquent, severe and useful to myself and others."

He refers to the "immortal abstracted pure friendships" of the Greeks, and gratifies the pedantry of
the Matchless Orinda by quotations from Theognis
and Theocritus, to which he is careful to append
translations of his own. In particular, he dwells
on that "commendation of the bravest friendship"
which he finds in the twelfth idyl, the 'Αἴτης, of the
Sicilian poet, part of which he turns into English
neatly enough: —

> "They loved each other with a love
>   That did in all things equal prove;
>   The world was under Saturn's reign,
>   When he that loved was loved again."

It is interesting, and characteristic of the exquisite tact
with which, in all his works, Taylor employs the honey
of the classics without a touch of their poison, that he

passes so deftly over the rather delicate ground involved in these citations.

But all his reflections have been leading him to
glorify the friendship of man with man. His gallantry
reminds him that Orinda's verses celebrate that of
woman with woman. He will not exclude this class
of emotion, though he thinks it rarer, and apt to be
more trivial and on a lower plane. Alas! if all could
share the transcendental raptures of the incomparable
Mrs. Philips, then indeed

> "twin souls in one should grow,
> And teach the world new love,
> Redeem the age and sex, and show
> A flame Fate dares not move."

But Taylor hints that his enthusiastic young correspondent has achieved this redemption, or is on the
high road to achieve it. Her example will show that
although a woman is not likely to prove so good a
counsellor as a wise man, she may be no less tender
and no less loyal. "A woman can love as passionately,
and converse as pleasantly, and retain a secret as
faithfully"; and "she can die for her friend as well
as the bravest Roman knight." It is hard if Mrs.
Philips was not satisfied with this. But her advocate
must guard and guide, so he proceeds to draw up a
code of laws, or maxims, for the prudent conduct of
friendship; and then sums up with a burst of emo-
tional eloquence not to be surpassed even in his
own writings : —

"As an eye that dwells long upon a star must be refreshed
with greens and looking-glasses, lest the sight become amazed
with too great a splendour, so must the love of friends sometimes be refreshed with material and low caresses. Lest by

striving to be too divine it become less human, it must be
allowed its share of both. It is human in giving pardon, and
fair construction, and openness, and ingenuity, and keeping
secrets. It hath something that is divine, because it is benefi-
cent, but much, because it is eternal. ''

It has been needful to dwell at some length on the
Discourse of Friendship, not merely because it is Taylor's sole contribution to secular literature, but because
it reveals to us sides of his character and temperament
which would otherwise be unknown. Sometimes, as
particularly in the rather harsh letter in which he
reproves, by implication, Evelyn's pride in the gardens
and buildings of Sayes Court, Jeremy Taylor faintly
repels us by an excess of sanctity. He seems a little
too seraphic for human nature's needs. He was a
firm and jealous guide of souls. But *A Discourse of
Friendship* survives to assure us of his geniality, his
acceptance of the social requirements of the creature,
and of his own participation in the unselfish joys of
life. Here he is neither mystical, nor sacerdotal.
Here he confesses to the weakness which longs for
comfort, to the depression of spirits which finds a
cure in friendly sympathy, to the attraction which
rests on no logical basis but is an instinct. He seems
to have read, and to have accepted, Montaigne's
phrase about La Boëtie: " Je l'aimais parce que
c'était lui, parce que c'était moi." The other writings
of Jeremy Taylor supply us with ample reason to
admire him ; the *Discourse* gives us authority to love
him.

Taylor was anxious that this treatise should not
pass into the wrong hands. He asked Orinda, if she
did not wish to publish it herself, to consign the MS.

to the keeping of Sir John Wedderburn. But she had no idea of wrapping up her treasure in a napkin; she published it immediately in folio. Wedderburn, who was "reckoned among his best friends" by Jeremy Taylor, was the great royalist physician of the day. He had attended Charles I. and he was useful to Charles II. before and after the Restoration. Although, or perhaps because, he made no secret of his ardent royalist proclivities, he amassed a large fortune during the Commonwealth. Anthony à Wood celebrates the Scotch doctor's noble hospitality and kindness to all who were learned and virtuous, and he was not only Taylor's intimate friend, but he attended him in each of his illnesses.

Although, from an obscure reference in a letter from Evelyn to the Governor of the Tower, it has been conjectured that in January 1657 Taylor for a third time suffered brief imprisonment, his position on the whole, though still perilous, was now less uncomfortable. We hear no more of grinding poverty; his subscriptions from the pious sufficed for his needs. English churchmen were now rigorously deprived of "the priest's power and external act," but persecution was more often threatened than carried out.

In May 1657 Taylor collected his works for the first time in a substantial folio volume; he continued to make efforts to publish his *Ductor Dubitantium*, and as Royston still shrank from so huge an undertaking, he proposed to print it at his own expense. He did not do this, but that he should have thought of doing it shows that he was no longer pressed for money. He was now the most popular theologian of the age, but he wrote little during these two years. He probably had no time for literature, for he was amply engaged by his mysterious occupations.

A glimpse of Jeremy Taylor in his pastoral capacity is offered us by his sermon preached at the funeral of Sir George Dalstone. This gentleman was a member of parliament from the county of Cumberland, who, being troubled by vexatious lawsuits, had given up the charge of his estates into the hands of his son, and had come up to London, where he devoted himself entirely to religion and philanthropy. He was in church one day, listening to the discourse, "for he was a great lover of sermons," when he was attacked by a paralytic seizure, and, being very old, was not expected to recover. Jeremy Taylor, who was probably the very preacher to whom he had been listening, was hastily called upon to attend him with the Holy Sacrament; it does not appear that they had ever spoken to one another before. But Sir George Dalstone did not immediately die, and during his last illness Taylor "often visited him," and found in him "a very quiet conscience." His decline was prolonged much beyond expectation, and through the course of it Taylor was greatly edified by the aged knight's serenity and beautiful attitude of readiness, and formed a very warm attachment to him. When at length Sir George Dalstone died, and was buried on the 28th of September 1657, Jeremy Taylor preached an unusually long and elaborate sermon at the funeral.

The nature of his clerical work seems to have been principally consultative rather than pastoral. He had a special charge to deal with persons who were tempted to change their religion, in particular, to join the Church of Rome. Some of his confidential letters to great ladies on points of conscience and delicate family matters have been preserved ; one of them, still among the Duke of Rutland's mss. at Belvoir, is addressed, in 1658, from Annesley to the Countess of Rutland. These letters hint at the personal risk Jeremy Taylor runs in carrying out his priestly task. He writes, for instance in 1657, " I bless God I am safely arrived where I desired to be after my unwilling departure from the place of your abode and danger." This is very cryptic, but it suggests the peril which attended one whose business in life it had become secretly to urge people to preserve the advantages of orthodox doctrine. But no further personal inconvenience seems to have attended him, until in 1658 he was translated to another and a fatal sphere of labour.

CHAPTER V

(1658–1661)

OF Edward, the third viscount (and afterwards first earl of) Conway, not much is preserved. But he was a pious and active Irish landlord, devoted to the Anglican church, and a convinced although not fanatical loyalist. He took his second title of Lord Killultagh from a district, " the woods of Ulster," in the south-western part of County Antrim, where his estates were bordered by Lough Neagh. His residence was called Portmore, in the parish of Ballinderry; it was a magnificent house, erected by the first viscount, after plans executed by Inigo Jones, and here Lord Conway resided in great state. The nearest town to him was Lisburn, or, as it was then called, Lismagarry, where there seems to have existed a collegiate church, in which the vicar taught divinity. This incumbent was a Presbyterian (or rather what was styled an Independent), but part of his fees, it would appear, were paid by Lord Conway and other subscribers, who therefore felt at liberty to exercise some pressure upon him. His name was Andrew Weeke, a man of some notable force of character, who had been minister of Lisburn since 1651. The attention of Lord Conway was drawn to the neglected state of the English church in that part of Ireland, and he formed the idea of inviting a leading churchman over to Lisburn to keep the flickering lamp of Anglicanism from being utterly extinguished.

Having consulted Evelyn, Lord Conway was advised to try and secure Jeremy Taylor, and in May 1658 he wrote to propose that the divine should accept the position of assistant lecturer at Lisburn. Unfortunately, the stipend offered was so inconsiderable, that it would not have paid for the expense and trouble of moving himself and his family to Ireland. Moreover, the idea of becoming a teacher under the disposal of a person like Andrew Weeke, who held views on church government diametrically opposed to his, was unwelcome to Taylor. He therefore desired Evelyn to give his thanks to Lord Conway, but to say that he declined the honour. In response to a further appeal, offering fresh inducements, Taylor asked Major George Rawdon, Lord Conway's brother-in-law, who commanded the garrison in Lisburn, for a frank account of the social conditions of that part of Ireland, and his reply was so extremely unfavourable that " it discouraged him and all his friends from any further thought of that country." Lord Conway, however, had thoroughly set his heart on securing Taylor, and in June he made a third attempt. He was " certain that [Taylor] was the choicest person in England appertaining to the conscience, . . . of excellent parts and an excellent life," and he was determined that come to Ulster he should. However, he was not blind to the difficulties, and he set about removing them on a large scale. As he admitted that Taylor's private virtues were not power-

ful enough "to purchase his quiet" in that bigoted
province, Lord Conway took infinite pains to protect
him.   He secured him, through William Petty and Dr.
Thomas Harrison, "a purchase of land at great advantage."   Dr. Thomas Coxe, afterwards president of the
College of Physicians, was induced to write and com-
mend Taylor "very passionately" to the Irish Chancellor.   Taylor was invited to come and converse with
Lord Conway during a visit the latter paid to Kensing-
ton, and in all possible ways was urged to try and
smile on the scheme.   Finally, the Lord Protector
was induced to give him a pass and a protection for
himself and his family, under his sign-manual and
privy signet.   The difficulty of the stipend was got
over, by the arrangement that he and his family were
to occupy rooms in the great house at Portmore, and
there was, without question, a salary offered as chaplain in Lord Conway's family.

   This last arrangement was against the law, and could
not be discussed in writing.   No doubt it was broached
when Taylor made his preliminary visit early in June
1658.   He yielded; Lord Conway had done so much
that it would have been ungracious to resist any further.   The viscount triumphed to his brother-in-law; he
recounted the infinite trouble he had taken, and added,
in reference to his success with Cromwell, "so that I
hope it will not be treason to look upon [Taylor] and
own him."   Accordingly, Jeremy Taylor's scruples
were removed, and before the summer of 1658 closed,
he and all his family removed from London to Portmore, to an asylum under the hospitable roof of Lord
Conway, who seems to have been proud of his company,
and always delicately solicitous as to his comfort and

safety. The quiet and repose were extremely welcome
to our author. He signs one of the very few letters
of this period " ex amœnissimo recessu in Portmore,"
" from my most delightful retreat." He left it, as is
supposed, once a week, to deliver his lecture in Lisburn,
which was but six Irish miles distant.

The only ambition Taylor had at this time was to be
let alone, to be undisturbed in his retreat. The recom-
mendations which his London friends had made on his
behalf to people in authority at Dublin were cunningly
devised to achieve this object. In the first place, he
was assured of the protection of " the Lord Peepes," in
whom we recognise Sir Richard Pepys, who had been
Lord Chief Justice of Ireland since 1654, and in contra-
vention to whose wishes no serious legal step could
be taken. But unfortunately Pepys died on the 2nd of
January 1659. Before coming to Ireland, Jeremy Taylor had formed what now proved a valuable friendship
with the eminent Irish orientalist, Dr. Dudley Loftus,
who was settled in Dublin as vicar-general and judge
of the prerogative court. Loftus, a fine scholar, though
it is said rather a flighty person, stood high in Cromwell's favour. Very important, too, was the protection
of Dr. Thomas Harrison, who must not be confounded
with the regicide. The former was the minister of a
dissenting chapel in Dublin, who had made himself
very prominent in politics, and who in 1657 went over
rather ostentatiously to Henry Cromwell's party. He
was rewarded by the governor's confidence, and his
advice was constantly asked for and acted upon. He
became almost a court chaplain in Dublin, and when
in 1658 he published his extremely successful manual
of piety called *Topica Sacra*, he was the most popular

divine in Ireland. This was a very valuable friend for
Jeremy Taylor to secure.

But among them all, probably none was so practically useful as Dr. (afterwards Sir William) Petty, the
great statistician and engineer. He had gone over to
Ireland in 1652, and had at once taken an interest in
the schemes for transplantation and the redistribution
of land. To him had been intrusted the famous
"Down" Survey of the whole of Ireland, and the map
in which he put the features "down" remains as a
monument to his industry. He was engaged for years
in delimiting the forfeited estates throughout Ireland,
and he had unrivalled opportunities not merely of
knowing where land was to be got, but of enabling
favoured persons to secure it on the most moderate
terms. It is likely that he enabled Taylor to buy the
farm at Magheralin, which he "provided" for him "at
great advantage," that is to say, for very little money
or for none at all. Experienced English farmers were
extremely welcome, and might almost be bribed to
settle. Magheralin is just within that portion of
County Down in which there were specially put aside
baronies to be divided among the disbanded soldiers
who were willing to settle. There can be little question that it was one of these which Petty secured for
Jeremy Taylor.

One friend at Dublin whom Taylor seems to have won
for himself, since this was one who was careful to display no political bias, was Dr. John Sterne, Archbishop
Ussher's grand-nephew. He was a very learned man,
a great doctor, and later on the founder of the Irish
College of Physicians. Sterne was certainly one of
the most accomplished persons then living in Ireland.

Although distinguished in science, he nourished a great fondness for theology, and this was the side of his character, no doubt, which attracted Taylor. A warm affection sprang up between them, and when Sterne published his *Thanatologia* in 1658, Taylor prefixed to it a long Latin epistle of congratulation and compliment. In 1660 Taylor was able to be of service to Sterne, by warmly recommending him, as a man of "great learning and skill in the college affairs," to Lord Ormonde for a senior fellowship at Trinity which was at the disposal of the chancellor.

Portmore is ignored by the guide-books, and its very site hardly remembered by the antiquaries, but in Jeremy Taylor's time it was, as has been said, the most magnificent mansion in Ulster. It stood on the western side of Lough Beg, a circular satellite of the vast Lough Neagh. At present it is difficult to find the remains of Portmore, but as the wanderer plashes about in the marshy flats, he becomes aware of a long line of broken brickwork on the crest of a slight eminence looking westward. This ridge, with what was evidently a bowling-green or garden in front of it, descending to the lake, marks the direction of the great terrace which rose from the plans of Inigo Jones soon after the rebellion of 1641. Portmore was not only a noble residence; it was a fortress garrisoned against the Tories of the west. Where now the eye perceives nothing but a low harsh horizon of grazing land to the north and east, in Lord Conway's time there lay a large deer-park of oak-trees. It is probable that a bridge, all traces of which have disappeared, conducted, in a few minutes from Portmore, across the brown and broad trout-stream, to the church in

which Jeremy Taylor habitually officiated. To reach
the latter now it is necessary to take a long, circuitous
route.   One arrives at last quite suddenly at its
impressive desolation.   It stands high on an artificial
island in the marshes, with a shallow moat encircling
it, although quite close to the banks of Lough Beg,
which are so low that the round lake looks like a
brimming cask buried in the soft soil. The fragments
of the church are covered heavily with ivy, and a loose
hedge of seedling larches and sweet-briar enrings them,
while here and there great cypresses, relics, it is possible, of the Italian gardens of Portmore, soar impres-
sively in the wild, bright place, where there has long
ceased to be heard any other sound than the cries of
wildfowl. From up among these ruins, the old fragmentary brickwork of Portmore is better visible than
from any other point, and imagination may here
rebuild the vision of it as Jeremy Taylor saw it when
he arrived in 1658, sumptuous and elaborate, with
its upper windows looking towards the sunset over
Lough Beg to the melancholy little inland ocean of
Lough Neagh. The church was dismantled by Taylor
himself, when he fitted up his new chapel in Ballinderry, just before his death. Portmore, after being
enlarged in 1664, lasted scarcely a century longer, and
was pulled down in 1761 after the extinction of the
Conway peerage.

Tradition will have it that the little Sallegh Island,
or isle of willows, which now lies a few hundred yards
out in Lough Beg directly north of Portmore, contained
a study where Jeremy Taylor loved to meditate. It has
been said that he wrote there in an "arbour," which
is probably a mere miscomprehension of his phrase

about Portmore itself, that it was his "harbour" or
asylum.   At present Sallegh Island, a tangled raft
of osiers, is unapproachable, and looks from shore as
though it were mere marshland.   It is probable, however, that while Portmore was a-building, there was
framed a little fort on Sallegh, and Taylor may have
fitted up a study there afterwards.   In the old (or
western) village of Ballinderry are one or two tall
warehouses, which probably belong to Lord Conway's
time.   The legend that Taylor wrote on Ram's Island,
far out in Lough Neagh, is preposterous.   All we can
safely say is, that he and his family occupied a suite
of rooms, from 1658 to 1660, in one of the wings of
Portmore, and that, doubtless, he stole away from the
noise of the great house to the islet which is now
sodden with rains, and to the church which is now two
gables of crumbling masonry.

The Presbyterian ministers, who had withdrawn
from persecution to Scotland, had come back to their
parishes in 1653 and 1654.   They were particularly
welcome in the Diocese of Down and Connor, where
they found a powerful patron in Lady Clotworthy,
mother of the first Lord Massereene.   "This poor
church," says Patrick Adair, had [in 1654] " a new
sunshine of liberty of all ordinances," and the Presbyterians flourished in the counties of Down and Antrim
for five years.   They were, however, vexed by the
existence of the Anabaptists on one side and by that
of Jeremy Taylor's Episcopal friends on the other, and
even their own partial historian admits that they were
divided amongst themselves by "some jealousies and
animosities."   To settle these internal factions and to
protect themselves against external enemies, the Pres-

156 JEREMY TAYLOR [CHAP.

bytery passed what was called "the Act of Bangor,"
which proved extremely consolidating, and enabled
them to carry out a detailed policy with great effec-
tiveness. "Even in the sight and to the angering of
their adversaries, the old Episcopal party and the
Anabaptists and other sectaries," the Presbyterians
succeeded in getting firm hold of the diocese. They
ruled it, indeed, with a rod of iron, tempered only by
the determination of Henry Cromwell to prevent all
overt acts of intolerance. But at the time of Jeremy
Taylor's arrival in Ireland, the attitude of the Presbyterians to Churchmen had grown as offensive as fear
of Cromwell would permit it to be. Those friends
of Taylor's whose names have been recounted were
prominent leaders of the Cromwellian party, who
were in favour of religious liberty, and who kept the
Presbyterians in check.

But three or four months after Taylor's arrival
the death of Oliver Cromwell (September 3, 1658)
altered the whole aspect of affairs. From having enjoyed a steady authority, the party of Henry Cromwell
in Ireland immediately became "staggering and reel-
ing." The Presbyterians in Down and Antrim lost no
time in taking advantage of the change, and they
adopted the double policy of intriguing for the king's
recall and of making the position of the Episcopalians
untenable. When, later on, we are confronted with the
undeniable, and much to be regretted, harshness of
Taylor as a bishop, it is only fair to remember that the
year 1659 was made intolerable to him by the enmity
which he met with from the surrounding ministers. It
is almost certain that the departure of Henry Cromwell
from Dublin was the signal of Taylor's dismissal from

his lectureship at Lisburn.   He withdrew altogether to
his retreat within the park of Portmore, and even there
it would seem that he was not safe from the insults of
the predominant party.   He kept close all the winter
of 1658–59, engaged in finishing *Ductor Dubitantium*,
which he hoped at length to see in the printer's hands,
although as a matter of fact its publication was again
delayed.   Colonel Hill, the strongest supporter of
Episcopacy in the county of Down, occasionally entertained him at his house in Hillsborough, and this seems
to have drawn the particular attention of the Presbytery to him.   A peculiarly busy fanatic, of the name
of Tandy, who divided his hostile attentions between
the Anabaptists and the Churchmen, became especially
offensive.   In June 1659 Taylor wrote Lord Conway,
who was in London, a letter which "almost broke his
heart."   Tandy had denounced Taylor to the Lord
Deputy and the council for illegal practices, and particularly for having baptized a child with the sign of
the cross.   Taylor was deeply alarmed, and expected
to be sent to prison.   Lord Conway wrote to Colonel
Hill, entreating him to protect the doctor so far as
his ability went, and forwarded a sum of money for
his legal defence.   Taylor was in despair; "I fear
my peace in Ireland is likely to be short," he wrote
to Evelyn, "for a Presbyterian and a madman have
informed against me as a dangerous man to their religion."   He hoped to be able to escape to England,
although he would fain stay where he is, "if I can
enjoy my quietness here."

The persecution, however, grew more intense, and
Taylor passed a distressing summer.   On the 11th of
August his calamities culminated in his arrest, at the

instance of Thomas Herbert, who directed Colonel
Bryan Smith, governor of Carrickfergus, forthwith at
sight to "cause the body of Dr. Jeremiah Taylor to
be sent up to Dublin under safe custody, to the end
that he may make his personal appearance before the
said Commissioners to answer unto such things as
shall be objected against him in behalf of the Commonwealth." We are told that the agitation of this
arrest and the subsequent enforced journey to Dublin
threw him into a serious illness; but this is perhaps
an echo of a later imprisonment. Dublin, however,
was not the County Down; the zeal of the Presbyterians was not greatly appreciated in the capital, and
here Taylor found a friend who had survived the fall
of the Cromwell party, Sir Matthew Thomlinson, a
leader of the military faction, whose attitude to Irish
politics was looked upon so unfavourably by the English Parliamentarians that an effort was now made to
impeach him. For a brief moment Thomlinson, who
was well affected to Jeremy Taylor, was one of the
most influential persons in Ireland.

Taylor seems not to have met with any harsh treatment in Dublin, and he returned to Portmore, where
he resumed his quiet life. But relations with England were disturbed; the postal system was entirely
dislocated, and he was left in anxiety about the condition of affairs. A reassuring letter from Evelyn,
sent off on the 23rd of July, was not delivered at
Portmore until the 1st of November. Taylor was
now, a second time, sent for to Dublin by the Commissioners, " in the worst of our winter weather," and
he " found the evil of it so great, that in my going I
began to be ill," and " in my return, had my illness

redoubled and fixed," so that it was not until February 1660 that his health was restored. He quite gave up all idea of remaining in Ireland, harassed as he was by the malevolence of the Presbyterian ministers, and he only waited for better weather "by God's permission to return to England." It was the darkest hour before the dawn. All this has been very slightly touched upon by those who have been only too ready to emphasise Taylor's subsequent rigour to the Presbyterians of his diocese. Without ceasing to regret that he did not see his way to treat them, in the hour of his authority, with greater indulgence, we must insist on pointing out how very offensive they had been to him, and to his fellow-churchmen, when Presbyterianism seemed to be enjoying a settled supremacy in Ulster.

When Jeremy Taylor, however, wrote the letter which has just been quoted, at the beginning of February 1660, the tide was flowing fast towards tolerance, for the new Convention, which had been called together in Dublin to replace the dissolved Irish parliament, was a complex body, in which, although the Presbyterians seemed predominant, the prelatical party had a great deal to say. As the restoration of the Stuarts became more and more certain, the ministers protested their fondness for the Royal family. But the Irish were suspicious, and Patrick Adair pathetically complains, "Yea, where a man was sober and godly, his loyalty was by the common sort of people more suspected." Meanwhile Jeremy Taylor was again in great poverty; if it had not been for a gift from Evelyn he could not have paid his debts. He was able, however, to pass through Dublin early in the spring, and to arrive in London in April. On the

24th of that month he affixed his signature to the dec-
laration of those leading loyalists who expressed their
satisfaction with Monk's policy and their confidence
in his judgment, and who declared for a constitutional
form of government.   Of Taylor's attitude at this
time, Rust gives an account, which no doubt gives a
very fair impression of the delirious excitement which
prevailed in the bosoms of all loyalists and churchmen.
" By this time the wheel of providence brought about
the King's happy restoration, and there began a new
world, and the Spirit of God moved upon the face of
the waters, and out of a confused chaos brought forth
beauty and order, and all the three nations were
inspired with a new life, and became drunk with an
excess of joy.   Among the rest, this loyal subject
[Jeremy Taylor] went over to congratulate the prince
and people's happiness, and bear a part in the universal
triumph."

On his passage through Dublin, Taylor had been
able to observe the astonishing improvement in the
prospects of his party, which the mere communication
with the King at Breda had brought with it.   If the
populace were sympathisers with the Presbytery, men
of light and leading were numerous on the Episcopal
side.   The stronger bishops, particularly Bramhall and
Henry Leslie, hastened to Dublin with, what their
antagonists lacked, a definite plan of campaign.   Leslie,
who throughout the troublous times had courageously
stuck to it that he was, by the grace of God and the
King, still Lord Bishop of Down and Connor, was in
close communication with Taylor.   Meanwhile, the
Presbyterians felt the lack of commanding personages
in their democracy.   One of the cleverest of them,

Patrick Adair, has described the condition of things in
mournful terms: "The Presbyterians had not men of
note and quality to be leaders in these affairs." Translated from their homes in Ulster, the ministers were
out of their element in Dublin, whither Adair himself
resorted to witness the melancholy change. "Our
grandees," he says, "began to court the few old
bishops who were in Ireland, and who had then
repaired to Dublin. They allowed them considerable
salaries in the meantime, and began to give them their
titles. . . . Some bishops who, at my arrival there,
had very hardly access to the Commissioners upon any
business, no one seeming to own them in the streets,
and who had been content with the countenance of
any private person, before I left [within three months
of his arrival] had become high, and much courted,
and their titles given them."

But Jeremy Taylor was now in London, and very
shortly after the King's arrival, giving his publisher
only just time to hurry through the press a jubilant
preface of welcome to "the most Sacred Majesty of
Charles II." he published at length the enormous work
on which we have seen him engaged at intervals for at
least twenty years. He had made effort after effort
to produce it before, but always without success. His
publisher was shy of so huge an enterprise; his fellow-
divines had eyed it with suspicion. That he could not
issue his great book of cases of conscience had been
the disappointment of his literary life. But now, as
he says, "our duty stands upon the sunny side"; anything published by the most eminent of living divines
was sure of a sale; and Royston hesitated no longer.
Jeremy Taylor, forever adding instances and heaping

M

up details, had come at last to the conclusion that his
book was finished. He may well have been put out
of countenance by the mountain of his manuscript.
On the 5th of October 1659 he closed the last sentence
of his preface in "my study in Portmore in Killultagh,"
although tradition asserts that the words were written
in a building on what is now the desolate islet which
has been described in Lough Beg. He decided on a
title at last, *Ductor Dubitantium, or the Rule of Conscience
in all her general measures.* He anticipated for his book
a universal welcome; this, or nothing, was to be his
masterpiece.

Posterity has refused anything more than respectful
recognition to the *Ductor Dubitantium.* Its bulk, its
want of variety, its utter discord with what we demand
in the form of theology, have left it to moulder on
high library shelves. But it has too hurriedly been
stated that it was a failure from the beginning.
Considered as an enterprise, Taylor's judgment was
justified as against the reluctance of Royston. It was
issued first in two folio volumes, then in one, and, costly
as it was, it was reprinted at least three times before
the close of the century. Of the bulk of the *Ductor,*
some impression may be formed from the fact that,
if printed from the same type, it would occupy some
twelve volumes equivalent to the present monograph.
This is a surprising amplitude for a treatise on the
conscience. But it must be recollected that it was
produced during an age of scruple, although, it is true,
towards the decline of that age. Taylor intended it,
too, to be, as far as possible, exhaustive. Moreover
there were still those alive who recollected the official
establishment which had been opened at Oxford for

the settlement of cases of conscience, and some who
would have welcomed the re-establishment of what
scoffers had called "the scruple-shop."

All through the early part of the seventeenth
century efforts had been made to compile a definitive
manual of Anglican casuistry. There had been felt
" a great scarcity of books of cases of conscience "; a
want not supplied by the innumerable expositions
and lectures of William Perkins, nor even by Joseph
Hall's *Resolutions and Decisions.* Taylor speaks of what
Hooker essayed to do; he does not mention what
Donne in one generation and Sanderson in the next
had planned. All had either sketched the work too
lightly, or had shrunk from its onerous elaboration.
Taylor attributed all these failures to the lack of that
psychological knowledge which experience only can
supply. " The careless and needless neglect of receiving private confessions hath been too great a cause of
our not providing materials apt for so pious and useful
a ministration." He speaks of " private conferences "
and of " admonitions and answers given when some
more pious and religious persons came to confessions,"
as the true preparation for such a manual of casuistical
theology. Well, perhaps no one else in that troubled
age had enjoyed exactly the same or anything like the
same advantages in this direction as Jeremy Taylor
had enjoyed in his confidential peregrinations. All
manner of strange scruples, all sophistications and
subtleties of conscience, all meanderings of souls to
whom life was " a wood before your doors, and a
labyrinth within the wood, and locks and bars to every
door within that labyrinth," had been submitted to
him in secret by anxious penitents, and for each his

lucid and ingenious spirit had devised some sort of
guidance.

The result of twenty years of cases noted in a succession of pocket-books, — that is the *Ductor Dubitantium ;* and it is hopeless to pretend that it offers a
vivid interest now to a generation which has shelved
its scruples altogether, or has generously simplified
them.   How can we excite ourselves to-day with a
discussion as to whether a man who has taken a vow
to abstain from wine may "nevertheless drink sherbets
and delicious beverages, strong ale and spirits"?
Although "a man is very much better than a beast,"
is not the life of a beast "better than the superfluous
hair of a man's beard"?   Common sense decides this
without casuistical effort.   Still more remote from us
is the inquiry whether "he that buys the body of a
slave hath right to all the ministries of his soul"?
A hospitably-minded Christian no longer rushes to his
parish priest to be told whether it is lawful to help an
honoured guest to get drunk at his table.   These seem
to us, what the still subtler hair-splittings of the Fathers
seemed to Taylor, "ridiculous commentaries and useless glosses."   They do explicit injustice to the intelligence and good sense which he rarely fails to display
in his commentaries, as where he openly declares that a
great deal that passes for scrupulosity of conscience is
nothing but the direct result of fatigue or ill-health.
His object is really to apply medicine to the morbid
nerves of his age.   He does not encourage useless
"tremblings"; he is distinctly averse to unnecessary
rules and the multiplication of unbearable burdens.
The *Ductor Dubitantium* is, in theology, very much
what Sir Thomas Browne's *Pseudodoxia Epidemica* is

in zoology. It is the work of a great modern spirit,
enlightened far beyond the average of his own day, yet
bearing about with him, and exhibiting on every page,
the evidences of the surrounding popular darkness.

In the course of a work from which — and this is one
great source of its tedium to-day — the autobiographical element is severely excluded, we come with pleasure on a single paragraph, which gives the general
reader all that he needs to know of Jeremy Taylor's
attitude towards his " cases of conscience " : —

" In hard and intricate questions I take that which is easy
and intelligible, and concerning which it will be easy to judge
whether it be right or wrong. In odious things, and matters
of burden and envy, I take that part which is least, unless
there be evident reason to the contrary. In favours, I always
choose the largest sense, when any one is bettered by that
sense, and no man is the worse. In things and matters
relating to men, I give those answers that take away scruples,
and bring peace and a quiet mind. In things relating to God
I always choose to speak that thing which to Him is most
honourable. In matters of duty I always choose that which
is most holy. In doubts I choose what is safest. In pro-
babilities I prefer that which is the more reasonable, never
allowing to any one a leave of choosing that which is con-
fessedly the less reasonable in the whole conjunction of
circumstances."

The pity of this lucid and admirably just summary
of the right temper of priestly sympathy is, that it
raises the question whether the conscience requires
more guidance than is, precisely in these sentences,
indicated ; whether, in short, from the practical point
of view, the remainder of the vast folio is not a super-
fluity. At the worst it is an entertaining miscellany
of stories and maxims, which might be read with pleas-

ure to-day, if it were not clogged with such masses of
Latin and Greek, and if it were not so interminably
lengthy. But there is another reason, and one too curious to be omitted, why the *Ductor Dubitantium* is no
longer to be recommended as a convenient guide for the
scrupulous. Jeremy Taylor's vast, confidential experience had proved to him how paramount a place is taken
by what he calls " odious things " in the scruples of the
sincere. The consequence is that the *Ductor Dubitantium* is crowded with considerations which a wise and
liberal-minded priest might discuss in private conversation with adult persons, but which must, one thinks,
even in 1660, have seemed indiscreet and embarrassing
when set down in print in a popular manual.

The saturation of Taylor's memory by the pagan
classics had given him a certain perduration of mind,
so that things which he sternly reproved, and most
sincerely abhorred, were yet no longer outside the
range of what he was prepared quietly to discuss. He
no longer discerned what things those are which it
is better that untrained consciences should not even
contemplate, nor realised that there are turpitudes
which demand silence more than exhortation. So
singularly large a place is taken by " odious things"
throughout the *Ductor*, that it would be disingenuous
not to face this characteristic, which is partly, of course,
but not at all entirely, common to the age in which
Taylor wrote. In all these matters, and in the treatment of other scruples of conscience, his absolute
mental aloofness is very interesting. He had the
judicial mind in its quintessence, and in practice must
have been the most imperturbable of confessors. Him,
at all events, we may without levity admit, no penitent

could "shock" out of his decorum. And throughout,
nevertheless, with his legal air of the tribunal, he
admits that in all things, within a certain oscillation
of the rules, each man is a law unto himself, and
truth itself not rigorously positive, but "like a dove's
neck or a changeable taffeta." It may be added that
if any reader desires to-day — no small adventure — to
read the *Ductor Dubitantium*, he may do so with profit
in the laborious edition brought out in 1851 by a
namesake of the author, the Rev. Alexander Taylor.

Charles II. arrived in London on the 29th of May
1660, and Taylor was one of those who took part in the
rapturous reception. Sixteen years had passed since,
as his father's domestic chaplain, Taylor had seen the
prince, and we may speculate in vain how the changes
in his appearance and demeanour struck him. This
was the moment when all lovers of Jeremy Taylor's
genius must unite in wishing that he had been encouraged to remain in England, but it is evident that
Bramhall, who was shortly nominated Archbishop of
Armagh, and Leslie, who was to be translated from
Down to Meath, must have represented that the presence of Taylor was essential to the wellbeing of the
Irish Church. Accordingly, on the 6th of August 1660
he was nominated, under the privy seal, to the vacant
bishopric of Down and Connor, and shortly afterwards,
on his way back to his see, was, at Ormonde's recom-
mendation, appointed vice-chancellor of the University
of Dublin. Although he did not take the oaths for the
latter office until early in 1661, he lost no time in
devoting himself to the labour of university reform.
On arriving in Dublin, he immediately set himself
to visit Trinity College, and on the 3rd of October

presented his first report to Lord Ormonde. He found
all the internal affairs of the University "in a perfect
disorder." The Provost was the only surviving relic
of the whole foundation, and it was necessary to set
aside all the usual methods of election to fill the vacant
fellowships.

He proposed, therefore, that a committee, consisting
of himself, James Margetson, Archbishop of Dublin,
as visitor, and the Provost of Trinity, should nomi-
nate seven senior fellows, three of whom, Dr. Sterne,
Joshua Cowley, and Patrick Sheridan, we know
to have been personal friends of Taylor's. Great
practical difficulties, however, intervened; Ormonde
was not willing to resign his own prerogative of
nomination, and it was not until December that "the
college was in its former state and possibility of
proceeding according to the elections." Just before
Christmas, Taylor laments that "we have no public
statutes relating to an university, no established forms
of collating degrees, no public lecturers, no schools, no
Regius professor of Divinity, and scarce any ensignes
academical." But gradually all these things were set
on foot, and it was not until he had seen "the university rising to its full state and splendour" that
he ventured to quit Dublin and proceed to his northern diocese. In his *Life of Ormonde*, Carte dwells on
Taylor's prodigious industry in collecting, arranging,
revising, and completing the body of statutes which
Bedell had left in confusion. But later writers have
hardly done justice to the extraordinary merit of
Taylor's labours in reconstituting the ancient centre of
Protestant learning in Ireland, when it had become a
mere "heap of men and boys, but no body of a college,

no one member, either fellow or scholar, having any legal title to his place." He carried out this great work, too, in the midst of distracting and humiliating interruptions of a most painful kind, for his nomination to the see of Down and Connor had been received with a storm of protest in the Ulster presbyteries. It should not be forgotten by us, what is doubtless well remembered in Trinity College, that Jeremy Taylor was the regenerating force which drew to one common system the scattered elements of Irish learning.

Late in the summer of 1660 Royston published another work of considerable importance by Jeremy Taylor, *The Worthy Communicant*. This was a treatise of a wholly uncontroversial character, composed in a spirit of serenity to which the author's conditions had long made him a stranger. It has been hastily described as written to instruct the newly victorious royalists in their duty to God. But careful examination will show that this is a mistake. Near the end of *The Worthy Communicant* we find the author speaking of the age in which he writes, as one where piety has suffered shipwreck, where all discipline has been lost in the storm, and where good manners have been thrown overboard. " The best remedy in the world that yet remains and is in use amongst the most pious sons and daughters of the church, is that they should conduct their repentance by the continual advices and ministry of a spiritual guide." These words evidently point to the time, from 1657 to 1659, when Jeremy Taylor was acting as a secret pastor, in the darkest hour, and among those who had still no hope of ecclesiastical restoration.

The advent of Charles II., however, offered him an
opportunity to bring forth his MS. and publish it.   It
is at any time a fatherly task for a divine to sum up
the duties of those who gather to receive the Holy
Communion.   Still, it is impossible not to see that
something of the appropriateness of this particular
treatise had passed away as soon as the embargo upon
public Anglican worship had been removed.   The
mystery, the air of ghostly comfort to a beleaguered
camp of the faithful, the unction of adversity, — these
are lost when all is prosperity and sunshine; and the
attitude of affliction seems misdirected when the long-
persecuted remnant are in the very act of being rewarded with posts of dignity and emolument.   Hence,
perhaps, although this is in some respects one of
Taylor's least-contestable works, it was never a great
popular favourite.   *The Worthy Communicant* was dedicated to the Princess Mary of Orange, the King's
sister.   This lady, who had been left a widow at
nineteen, had developed a strong character.   A convinced Protestant in spite of all the pressure towards
Rome brought to bear upon her by her mother, Queen
Henrietta Maria, she had become a particular patron
of English divinity.   Her court in Holland "hath
been in all these late days of sorrow a sanctuary to
the afflicted, a chapel for the religious," and it was
hoped that her arrival in England would be of good
omen for the English Church.

Princess Mary of Orange was a great admirer of
Taylor's genius.   She "read and used divers of my
books," he says.   He had not seen her since she was
a child of twelve, and he was disappointed of resuming
an acquaintance which would now have been of great

value to him. The Princess delayed her coming, and before she arrived, on the 30th of September, Taylor's duties had called him back to Ireland. Her visit to England was ill-starred in the highest degree; she was displeased with many things, her health failed, and on the 24th of December she died, only twenty-nine years of age, leaving behind her, besides a reputation for piety and for something of the family obstinacy, a child who was destined to be King William III. It is almost certain that if the Princess had remained at the court of Whitehall, she would have insisted on securing for Jeremy Taylor promotion to one of the great English sees for which his loyalty, his eloquence, and his unrivalled reputation so manifestly designed him.

Towards the close of *The Worthy Communicant* Jeremy Taylor uses words which accurately sum up the scope of that book. " Every worthy communicant," he says, " must prepare himself by a holy life, by mortification of all his sins, by the acquisition of all Christian graces. And this is not the work of a day, or a week; but by how much the more these things are done, by so much the better are we prepared." The treatise is non-contentious; its tone is gentle and persuasive. It is a discourse of the nature and uses of the Lord's Supper, " the blessings and fruits of the Sacrament," and of how we must initiate ourselves into them. It is, in short, a manual of conduct in these solemn circumstances; it contains many wise and beautiful reflections, might be shredded into an anthology of maxims, and is interspersed, after Jeremy Taylor's favourite fashion, with exquisitely fervent prayers. " The fierce saying of a few warm and holy words is not a sufficient preparation to these sacred mysteries," and we are, throughout, in the presence of one who is deeply solicitous for the persistent holiness of the souls to whom he is the guide. Ever-recurring are Taylor's extreme solicitude about the importance of vital repentance, and about the necessity of keeping the conscience sensitive and sound.

From a literary point of view, *The Worthy Communicant* exhibits the natural, we may almost say the physical, progress of its author's mind. It is marked by strength and warmth of expression, and by an absence of all oddity of verbiage. The style is perfectly pure and simple, clarified by maturity and experience. At the same time the rich perfume of the Golden Grove period seems to have evaporated. The images taken from external nature have almost disappeared. The apologues are still beautifully told, but without audacities of phrase; they are told in a new way, which leans towards the coming Eighteenth Century. Many pages here, in their lucidity, without colour or picturesqueness, might almost be the writing of Tillotson, so reasonable and succinct are their constructions. So that we see, in this book, the genius of Jeremy Taylor unconsciously responding to the appeal of European taste, and adapting its step to the fashion of the times. But already how far are we from the splendour of the great period, while in exchange for correctness and sobriety of style we have parted with a charm that now never can return. This estimable book consoles us for the fact that events now interrupted and presently closed the life of Taylor as a man of letters, since it shows us that what we love best in his writing, its rapturous mounting note, had departed from it for ever.

Jeremy Taylor was not left under any illusion as to

his welcome in County Down. A preliminary visit to
his intended diocese filled him with alarm and disappointment. In the face of impending events, his
first impressions, as reported to Ormonde in a letter
of December 19, 1660, deserve our careful notice : —

"His sacred Majesty and your Excellence intended to
prefer me, in giving me the bishopric of Down. But, —
besides that I find it very much short of what it was represented to me, and much of the rents litigious and uncertain,
of which I will not complain, — I perceive myself thrown into
a place of torment. The country would quickly be very well,
if the Scotch ministers were away, at least some of the prime
incendiaries. All the nobility and gentry, one only [Lord
Massereene] excepted, are very right, but the ministers are
implacable. They have for these four months past solemnly
agreed, and very lately renewed their resolution, of preaching
vigorously and constantly against episcopacy and liturgy. . . .
They talk of resisting unto blood, and stir up the people to
sedition. . . . They have now gone about to asperse me as an
Arminian, and a Socinian, and a Papist, — or at least half a
Papist, . . . and I am not at all guilty, as having no other
religion but that of the Church of England, for which I have
suffered the persecution of eighteen years. . . . But yet they
have lately bought my books, and appointed a committee of
Scotch spiders to see if they can gather or make poison out of
them, and have drawn some little thing, I know not what, into
a paper, and intend to petition to his Majesty that I may not
be their bishop."

It is amusing to see an amiable inconsistency
between Taylor's anger at "Scotch spiders" buying
his books, and his advice, given a few days later,
to a fellow of Trinity of the name of Graham,
who asked for a list of the best existing works on
practical theology, perhaps for the College Library.
In the latter case, Taylor cheerfully supplied a brief

catalogue of publications which "he that would improve in the doctrine of the Church of England" must "be very perfect in every part of"; and there is scarcely a book or a pamphlet which Taylor had ever printed which does not appear somewhere or other on this list. Meanwhile his complaint to Ormonde was perhaps a little more tragical than the circumstances demanded, although these were awkward enough. He went down from Dublin to preach every Sunday somewhere or other in his future diocese, and had already made a good impression upon the affections of "the gentry and the better sort of the people." Among the non-Presbyterian part of the population he met with universal esteem. Unhappily, of course, it was precisely the Presbyterians who were vastly in the majority, and Jeremy Taylor was forced to the conclusion that their ministers, at least, were implacable. His report of their rejection of his advances is not to their credit. The bishop wrote: —

"They threaten to murder me. They use all the arts they can to disgrace me, and to take the people's hearts from me, and to make my life uncomfortable and useless to the service of his Majesty and the Church. . . . It were better for me to be a poor curate in a village church than a bishop over such intolerable persons; and I will petition your Excellence to give me some parsonage in Munster, that I may end my days in peace, rather than abide here, unless I may be enabled with comfort to contest against such violent persons. . . . My charge hath in it more trouble than all the dioceses in his Majesty's dominions put together."

He was quite sincere in wishing to withdraw from Down and Connor. He begged Ormonde to let him come back to Dublin and devote himself entirely "to

the service and resettling of the University," which
still required great care and labour. When the government merely smiled, and said that he must stay in
Ulster and do his best, Taylor replied that in that case
he must be assisted by the secular arm. Ormonde
then signified that the bishop would receive full support in doing his duty, and that he must not take
such a despairing view. If the Scotch spiders were
sulky, he must handle a long broom and sweep them
out of their webs. Accordingly, he took what heart
he could, but he had no peace or happiness all the
time that he was bishop in Down; and there can be
no question that the constant friction with his Presbyterian neighbours, and those "insufferable discour-
agements" of which he never ceased to complain,
paralysed his usefulness and shortened his life.

The ecclesiastical arrangements for the filling of the
Irish sees were not finally completed until the 18th of
January 1661, when two archbishops and ten bishops
were instituted in St. Patrick's Cathedral. John
Bramhall, now Archbishop of Armagh, in succession
to Ussher, who had died five years before, presided
at the consecration, and Jeremy Taylor preached the
sermon. Old Henry Leslie, who was in his eighty-
first year, was transferred from Down and Connor to
Meath, and Jeremy Taylor took his place. Robert
Leslie, who "was nothing short of his father in
cruelty to Nonconformists, but rather exceeded him,"
went to Dromore. It was in these contiguous Ulster
dioceses that the Presbyterians were strongest, and
"there were not three such bishops in Ireland"
for the stringency of their Episcopalianism. It is
melancholy to have to record that even Bramhall,

who was called " the Irish Laud," did not contrive to
vex the souls of the Presbyterian ministers so much
as did the author of the *Liberty of Prophesying*. Taylor was but carrying out, however, the theories of his
predecessor, Henry Leslie, who had compared the
Independents and the Presbyterians to the thieves
between whom our Lord was crucified.

Jeremy Taylor's headquarters when he first took up
the labours of his diocese was Hillsborough, where he
is believed to have occupied rooms, with his family, in
" the noble large house," fitted up as a regular fortress,
which had been built and manned by Colonel Arthur
Hill. There is no other place in Ireland where the
impression of Taylor's daily life can be reconstructed
with so great a measure of success as it can at Hillsborough. The castle of the Hills had been built on
the abrupt eminence of Crumlin, by Colonel Hill during the reign of Charles I., as an outpost against
the rebels of the west. It was accidentally burned
down, in main part, early in the eighteenth century,
and the family then removed to the great house, a
little to the west, which is still the residence of the
Marquis of Downshire. But enough is left of the old
fortress to permit us to restore the general plan of its
construction. A little ecclesiastical building, ruined
but still largely intact, on the ring of wall, was doubtless the chapel in which Jeremy Taylor officiated.
To this day the traces of buildings around the courtyard are brought to light whenever the spade is used,
and before any town existed the whole life of the
place was included within their circle.

The pretty and neat little borough town, very English in character, which now struggles up the steep

rock from the north, cannot have existed in the seventeenth century; it dates from about 1750. But there
may have been a rude village lower down, where, at
the bridge, there stood a small parish church when
Taylor first came to Hillsborough. This was falling
into ruins, and in 1662 the bishop and Colonel Hill
constructed, a few yards from the old castle and
almost within its precincts, a spacious, well-contrived
church, dedicated to St. Malachy, in the form of a
cross, on the very brow of the hill. This, which was
called Jeremy Taylor's church, was rebuilt and much
enlarged, after a fire, in the eighteenth century, and
all that remains of it is the base of one of the outer
walls built into the present edifice.

It has quite recently (1903) been discovered by
Canon Lett of Loughbrickland, the distinguished antiquary, that Homra House, a little solitary mansion two
miles to the west of Hillsborough, just off the road to
Comber, belonged to Jeremy Taylor, and that in the
later part of his life the prelate often resided there.
He is also said to have occupied, and even to have
built, a house in Castle Street, Lisburn, opposite the
door of the church which then served as cathedral to
the united dioceses. It was, however, a very short ride
from Hillsborough to Lisburn, and it is most reasonable
to suppose that the bishop mainly resided, at all events
at first, in the castle at Hillsborough, where he was
safer than anywhere else in his diocese from the enmity
of his Presbyterian ministers, and from their petty
annoyances. In Lisburn, although its cathedral, with
a tower and an octagonal spire, may vaguely remain
the same, there is little else to recall the seventeenth
century. That town was destroyed by fire early in the

N

nineteenth, and has scarcely an old house in it. The traveller, however, who follows the undulating road between Lisburn and Hillsborough, is on a track which must have been incessantly traversed by the bishop, as he rode from his castle to his cathedral church; and the general aspect of the brisk, rolling landscape has probably changed but little in two centuries and a half. It has, however, changed in one particular which must not be forgotten. As Lord Londonderry said in a recent speech, the county of Down, which is now the richest in Ireland, was, at the Restoration, perhaps the poorest.

It was in a spirit grievously exasperated against the rebellious shepherds of his flock that, in March 1661, Jeremy Taylor made his first visitation. He sent before him into Antrim and Down a proclamation from the Dublin courts of justice, discharging all Presbyterian meetings. The terrified ministers, at his approach, hurriedly met in synod at Ballymena. A troop of horse was sent by Taylor's friend, Sir George Rawdon, to disperse them, but they had concluded their meeting before the troopers arrived. They forwarded a deputation of their body to Dublin to plead their cause before Lord Ormonde. Jeremy Taylor immediately left for the north, having received an assurance that no encouragement would be given to the ministers. He waited at his apartments in Hillsborough until they returned home, and then summoned them all to meet him at Lisburn. Meanwhile, at this peculiar juncture, their principal patron, Lady Clotworthy, died, and at her funeral, which took place at Belfast the day before that which the bishop had fixed for the visitation, the ministers took counsel together. Then and there

they sent three of their number to Hillsborough, to
tell Jeremy Taylor that they did not acknowledge his
Episcopal jurisdiction, and should not appear next day
in answer to his summons.

It does not seem that he treated the representative
ministers, for this act of extreme insubordination,
with severity. He told them that if they would define
their position on paper, he would discuss it with them.
He then asked them whether they considered the
Presbyterian form of government exclusively the right
one, and *de jure divino*. They said at once that they
did. It is not easy to see what else they could say,
but on the other hand it made compromise impossible.
The bishop was left in the dilemma that he must
either subdue the ministers, or resign his see. This
he pointed out to them, and added " that there needed
no further discourse of the matter of accommodation,"
if they held to their unyielding position. They professed that they were willing to discuss their views in
public at the visitation, but the bishop naturally felt
that it was impossible to allow that. Taylor's patience
seems to have broken down, and he sharply instructed
them that " if they should make profession contrary
to law at the visitation, they would smart for it."
Then, speaking more gently, he advised them, as
a friend, not to attempt to justify their position
by argument. But in the subsequent conversation,
much bad blood was stirred on both sides, and we
do not recognise our gentle Taylor, although we have
had experience of his obstinacy, when he told his
visitors, who hesitated about the Oath of Supremacy,
that they " were the greatest enemies to monarchy, and
most disobedient to kings, which he instanced in the

case of the Assembly of Scotland, and in Calvin, Knox, and Buchanan." He compared them with the Jesuits, and they returned, greatly troubled at their reception, to their brethren, who had meanwhile collected at Lisburn, but who now, on hearing the report of their friends, dispersed to their parishes.

When Taylor arrived at Lisburn next day, and found that only two of his entire clergy had responded to his summons, he was very angry. We must admit that he had cause for his vexation. Those who have blamed him have hardly, it seems to me, taken into due consideration the humiliating *impasse* in which the rigidity of his opponents placed him. They would neither go to him nor leave him alone. He had hardly retired to his house in Hillsborough when another deputation of ministers waited upon him. He asked them why they had treated him with so much contempt by not coming to his visitation. They replied "it was the awe of God and conscience that made them not appear." Seeing that he could obtain no concession of any kind from the deputation, he dismissed them ; but he called several of them to him in private, and spoke to them, as they admitted, with the greatest kindness and indulgence. But, says Patrick Adair, grimly, "he obtained not his purpose," and they repaired to their respective congregations in a state of open rebellion. The plan of the ministers can easily be comprehended ; they aimed at making the diocese of Down and Connor one which it was impossible for a bishop of the Church of England to hold. They thought that by acting in unison, and by refusing to recognise Jeremy Taylor's authority in any way, and by hinting broadly about " resisting unto blood," they

would so distress and intimidate the bishop that he
would retire, and leave Ulster to the undisputed sway
of the Presbytery. They had seen that he was a gentle,
sensitive, and kind-hearted man, and they thought that
they could break down his nerves.

But the Presbyterian ministers reckoned without a
quality in Jeremy Taylor's character, to which we have
several times referred, namely, his obstinacy. Timid
and tractable as he was, there was easily reached a
point in controversy with him where he suddenly
refused to yield a step further. Before his visitation
at Lisburn, and at the mere thought of having to
face the "dour" ministers, he had passed through an
agony of trepidation. But when once their will had
clashed with his, he recovered his moral equilibrium.
If we look at the events, not in a party spirit, with
a leaning to either side in religion or politics, but as
at a human spectacle, I know not how we can refuse
our admiration to Jeremy Taylor when he now turns,
and, standing almost alone, a stranger and an English-
man in this fanatical diocese, defies the whole body of
his unscrupulous foes. He saw that the moment for
weakness was past. The Presbyterian ministers had
openly risen in revolt against him, and it was necessary to choose between crushing them and being
crushed by them. If he chose the latter, he betrayed
the Church and the King, his own principles, the
populations among whom he had been sent as a shepherd. He did not hesitate a moment; he immediately declared thirty-six parishes vacant, and filled
these incumbencies with clergy whom he invited out
from England. What with these, and with the curates
who accompanied them, Taylor brought over quite a

large ecclesiastical colony, and one of these emigrants, the excellent George Rust, he appointed Dean of Connor. The work of turning out the Presbyterian ministers, who struggled to retain their parsonages "till it became physically impossible for them to continue," of installing and protecting the new clergy, of conciliating the congregations, of exhorting and cheering and rebuking his flock in all corners of the diocese, of deciding cases where, as at Killead and Antrim, the ministers could safely be allowed a six months' grace, — all this occupied Jeremy Taylor through the stormy year 1661. Throughout it was a painful business, involving bitterness and exasperation; but all the evidence, and it is mainly on the Presbyterian side, goes to prove that the bishop carried out his distasteful duty with firmness and courage, and, superficially at least, with not a little success. The diocese, at all events, became quiet, and the Episcopalian form of worship established.

Taylor often lost hope, however, and he was never happy in County Down. At the end of March 1661, when he had resided there only a couple of months, he begged that if the aged Henry Leslie should die, he might be translated to the diocese of Meath, which would be much more convenient for his duties in Dublin, since he was now not merely vice-chancellor of the University, but a member of the Irish Privy Council. He wrote to Ormonde: "Here I am perpetually contending with the worst of the Scotch ministers. I have a most uncomfortable employment, but, I bless God, I have broken their knot, I have overcome the biggest difficulty, and made the charge easy for my successor." To Taylor's extreme disappoint-

ment, when Leslie died, on the 9th of April 1661, Henry
Jones, the veteran bishop of Clogher, was appointed to
the vacant diocese, and it was again indicated to Taylor
that he must stay where he was.   Doubtless he felt that
it was unreasonable to take his hand from the plough
so soon, for we hear no more complaint from him for
some years.   Meanwhile he laboured in the thorny
field, and in such a manner that Rust, speaking to
those who had been most closely associated with him,
could say " with what care and faithfulness he dis-
charged his office, we are all his witnesses."

CHAPTER VI

(1661–1667)

JEREMY TAYLOR is often described as " Lord-Bishop of Down, Connor, and Dromore," and this is even the style which his editor and biographer, Heber, gives him on the title-page of the *Whole Works*. He seems to have been, however, at no time Bishop of Dromore, although, after the early months of 1661, that diocese became a very important centre of his activities. Dromore was a bishopric founded by St. Colman in the sixth century, but its independent existence in post-Reformation days began when James I. severed it from the diocese of Down, in which it had been merged. It was at first a small cluster of parishes in the western part of the county, and contained, at the Restoration, only five incumbencies, together with several " dignities of the church," which made a great strain upon its slender revenues. The rebellion of 1641 had utterly ruined it. Buckworth, the bishop, had just completed, at great expense, a palace close to the cathedral, and this, with every building in the town, was burned by the Tories. When Jeremy Taylor arrived at Hillsborough, and rode over to Dromore, which is only four English miles to the south of that

184

fastness, he found a poor cluster of huts beginning to struggle up the hill from the river Lagan, but no attempt made to restore the charred ruins of the cathedral.

The diocese of Dromore was practically bankrupt, and Taylor received a deputation from the neighbouring nobility and gentry, proposing that it should be merged once more in Down and Connor. It was, as he told Ormonde, "not of extent or charge enough for a bishop," and on the 28th of March 1661, when Henry Leslie lay a-dying, Taylor, as we have seen, applied to the government that he should be translated to Meath, and that the united northern diocese should be resigned to Robert Leslie, who would then be bishop, not merely of Dromore, but of Down and Connor as well. It is unfortunate that this arrangement was not carried out, for in Meath Taylor would not only have been placed in the midst of a friendly population, but he would have been close to Dublin and to his valuable work at Trinity College. Ormonde, however, would not hear of it, but Robert Leslie was translated to Raphoe, and on the 30th of April Taylor was appointed by royal letter "administrator" of the diocese of Dromore. The plan was, by temporarily suspending the election of a bishop to that see, to give it a sort of minority, during which it could recover its solvency. This seems to have been fairly acceptable to Jeremy Taylor, who received, not indeed an Episcopal salary, but considerable fees for his administration, and Dromore had no bishop until, in 1667, George Rust was appointed. The writ under the privy seal sets forth that the stewardship was given to Taylor "on account of his virtue, wisdom, and industry." He seems to have administered the revenues of the see with unusual dexterity, and to have placed Dromore on a prosperous footing.

One of the first things he did was to raise a cathedral on the site of the church which the rebels had destroyed. He built a small and decent edifice, not constructed in the form of a cross, but consisting of a nave with a choir which he added at his own expense. It is to be regretted that Dromore, with which Jeremy Taylor was so closely identified, now offers the visitor very little indeed which can be connected with him. The small grey town seems to contain not a single house which is not long subsequent to Taylor's death. The two-arched bridge over the river may be one of his constructions. The palace, now (1903) unoccupied, on the hill to the north-west of the station, is quite modern; probably the ruined palace was not rebuilt in Jeremy Taylor's time. Even the cathedral, reconstructed rather than restored, is most disappointing, and a certain amount of basal masonry is all that has survived of the church which he built in 1661. We shall speak later on of such relics of Taylor as the present cathedral contains. It would be useless to search for any traces of his residence in Dromore, since it is certain that he administered the little diocese from his apartments in Hillsborough Castle.

We hear extremely little of Jeremy Taylor's family life in Ireland. His son Edward, perhaps his only son by his wife Joanna, was buried at Lisburn on the 10th of March 1661; he could not have been more than five years old at the time. There is evidence that through the year 1661 Taylor was making what proved a hopeless struggle to keep up

his intimacy with his old English friends. It is a
very pathetic fact that after this date their names
disappear from his correspondence. The distance
between Ulster and London was great, and methods
of communication were primitive and slow. The new
conditions introduced into English life by the Restoration gave every one a great deal to think about; leisure
was restricted, and business vastly increased. When
Jeremy Taylor went over to London to welcome
Charles II., he had renewed his friendship with his
old patron, Lord Hatton of Kirby, and many memories
had been awakened in his bosom. When he returned to
Ireland he hoped that Lord Hatton, although time and
misfortune had greatly changed him, would continue
their former correspondence, but the peer had other
matters on his mind. Taylor tried to fancy that his
own importunate letters had "some way or other mis-
carried," but Lord Hatton was obstinately mute. "If
I might have leave, and knew how, whither, and in
what circumstances to address my letters to your
Lordship, so that they might come readily to your
hand," the bishop wrote on the 23rd of November, "I
would write often, for though I be a useless person,
yet nobody loves and honours my dear Lord Hatton
so much as I do"; but Ireland was a long way off, and
he was not encouraged to persevere.

Nor was his experience any better with a dearer and
a better friend, Evelyn, to whom Jeremy Taylor wrote
in the course of the same week. "I pray you let me
hear from you as often as you can, for you will very
much oblige me if you will continue to love me still."
He confesses "I am so full of public concerns and the
troubles of business in my diocese, that I cannot yet

have leisure to think of much of my old delightful
employment" of writing letters to Evelyn. But "I
hope I have brought my affairs almost to a consis-
tence," and then, surely, the friends may begin again
on the former pleasant footing of mutual correspondence and intimacy. Evelyn sends him some printed
tracts, but no more letters, and he too drops noiselessly
out of the affectionate bishop's life. It is the same
with "worthy Mr. Thurland," although Taylor tries
to excite him by the transmission of "my love and
dear regards." He had to be content with new faces
and the Irish intimacies; a curtain fell between
England and his home-sickness. It was not that the
hearts there had grown cold to him; but he was as
distant from their interests then, as he would be from
ours to-day in Madagascar or the Falkland Islands, and
he had to be content, like exiles all the world over,
with the conviction that his friends would still love
him — if they could only recollect him.

Jeremy Taylor was now recognised as by far the finest
orator in Ireland, and was indispensable upon great occasions. For his sermon, preached at the opening of
Parliament on the 8th of May 1661, he received the
thanks of both Houses, and its publication was ordered.
The preacher hesitated to obey; but when it was
represented to him that what he had so brilliantly
said would otherwise fade from the memory of
those who listened to it, he replied, "I would not
shed that chalice which my own hands have newly
filled with waters issuing from the fountains of
salvation," and consented. In the preface to this
sermon he complains that his "eyes are almost grown
old with seeing the horrid mischiefs which come from

rebellion and disobedience." But so far as bowing
the head goes, he is determined to be firm. He will
not be one of those weak brethren " who plead for toleration and compliance," and he lets it be known, in
the clearest possible tones, that he means to impress
the law against the Presbyterian " wild asses in the
wilderness." His sermon at the opening of Parliament
is one of his cleverest and most trenchant minor
writings, admirably colloquial, and even, at times,
humorous. The line of argument is that there can be
no happiness and no prosperity for the troubles of
Ireland, unless she is docile. It is the duty of
Parliament to enforce docility. "God hath put a
royal mantle, and fastened it with a golden clasp,
upon the shoulder of the King; and He hath given
you the judge's robe; the King holds the sceptre, and
he hath now permitted you to touch the golden ball."
He promises that the bishops will be firm in doctrine,
if the Houses will be equally firm in law, and together
they shall proceed to the salvation of Ireland. Above
all things, he deprecates " a pitiful, a disheartened, a
discouraged clergy, that waters the ground with a
waterpot, here and there a little." The sermon is
a very strong document, which must have encouraged
the government greatly in its task. We have only to
read it to comprehend the sensation which it produced
and the enthusiasm which it awakened. It marks the
moment of Jeremy Taylor's highest complacency about
his work in Ulster, when he was flushed with his original triumph, and had not experienced the reaction.

Another publication of 1661 was the *Via Intelli-
gentiæ*, an expansion of an address first delivered to
the University of Dublin, and afterwards, in a modified

form, to the clergy of Taylor's diocese during a metropolitan visitation which the Archbishop of Armagh, the aged John Bramhall, made in the summer of 1661. Taylor had now collected his imported clergy from England, and they rallied about him and about the Primate in a highly gratifying manner. There was, we are told, "a clergy-show," and after it a banquet was given by Taylor, probably at Hillsborough, in honour of Bramhall, and the party is described as an extremely successful one. The newly appointed incumbents learned to know one another, and to see their bishop in the light of an assiduous and generous host. They might also admire, not without a touch of awe, the "stupendous parts, and mighty diligence, and unusual zeal" of the not a little formidable Primate, who was fighting still, "only mortality was too hard for him," and years beginning to tell upon the fierceness of his energies. Before the "excellent dinner" was served, Jeremy Taylor preached to the assembled Primate and clergy, and all the gentry that had come to his table, a sermon which he presently published and distributed.

If 1661 was a very full year in the history of Jeremy Taylor, 1662 is marked only by anecdotes. As we have already seen, he was inclined to a moderate credulity about the spirit-world. He has been unjustly accused of believing grossly in ghosts; it would be more just to say that he was in favour of psychical research. He was now thrown into the midst of a very superstitious population, and he was by no means helpless, though vividly curious, in presence of their tales of wonder. Late on the night of Michaelmas 1662, a porter called Francis Taverner, who had been at Hillsborough, was riding to his house near Belfast, when he came to the Drum bridge, which crosses the Lagan at Drumbeg. He was "a lusty proper stout fellow," about twenty-five years of age. At the foot of the bridge his horse stopped suddenly; Taverner dismounted, urged the beast forward, and as he started again, was aware of two shadowy horsemen who rode beside him, like the great Twin Brethren by the shore of Lake Regillus. At the same moment a third man, in a white coat, was at his elbow, and, turning, Taverner perceived that this resembled one James Haddock, who had died five years before. Taverner asked the apparition who in the name of God he was. Haddock told his name, and bade him not be afraid, reminding him of a trivial circumstance, how Taverner had brought some nuts to Haddock and to the two friends who were now noiselessly riding on before them. A brief conversation brought the party to four cross roads, where the path from Dunmurray to Lismoyne crosses the Belfast road. Here the ghost desired the young man to turn aside with him, but Taverner would not, and, galloping on, left him there. Whereupon "there arose a great wind, and withal he heard very hideous screeches and noises, to his amazement." But presently morning broke, the cocks crew, and, slipping off his horse, Taverner knelt in prayer to God, and so came safely to Belfast.

Next night, as he sat by the fire with his wife, the ghost of Haddock appeared to him again, and sent a vague message about a will and a lease to a certain widow, Eleanor Welsh, at Malone, a hamlet close by, where Taverner's family lived. This message would have upset the whole neighbourhood, and Taverner

could not bring himself to give it. Night after night
the ghost appeared, more and more importunate and
angry, now when the porter was sitting at the hearth,
now when he was in bed. It was never visible to
Mrs. Taverner, although she was a terrified witness of
her husband's agitation. For a whole month James
Haddock, in a white coat, haunted the unfortunate
young man, who, to escape from the visitation, left
his home in the hills, and took refuge with a shoe-
maker in Belfast; but all in vain. The story gradually
filled the whole country-side, and reached the bishop,
who was holding his court in Dromore.

Thomas Alcock, Jeremy Taylor's secretary, who
has preserved the story, was instructed to send for
Taverner, as the bishop was extremely interested in
what he called "this strange scene of Providence."
He held a judicial inquiry at Dromore, and cross-
examined, not Taverner only, but various other
witnesses who were collected for the purpose. The
young porter's evidence was not shaken, and Taylor
came to the conclusion that this was a genuine instance
of the apparition of the souls of the dead. Lady
Conway, a learned blue-stocking whose headaches
were among the most celebrated indispositions of that
day, and who affected a universal intellectual curiosity,
asked to have the case retried for her benefit at Hillsborough, which Taylor, taking Taverner and all the
witnesses over from Dromore, actually did before a
fashionable company. The bishop then supplied
Taverner with a set of questions, which he was to
put to the ghost, if it appeared again; and at night
sent him off to Lisburn, where he was put up in Lord
Conway's house. There Taverner and his brother were

in the courtyard, when the former saw the spectre in
its white coat come over the wall to them. Taverner
plucked up courage and asked his set of questions, but
the ghost "gave him no answer, but crawled on his
hands and feet over the wall again, and so vanished
in white, with a most melodious harmony." And that
was the close of the incident. But that it was a true
story of a real ghost, "all wise and good men did
believe, especially the bishop, and Dr. Rust, the Dean
of Connor."

We possess the questions which Jeremy Taylor
proposed to the ghost, and they are of a nature to
suggest that in his judgment it might be a spirit of
evil masquerading in Haddock's shape. Among the
questions was this: "Why do you appear in so small
a matter, when so many widows and orphans in the
world are defrauded of greater matters?" This is
exactly in the spirit of Huxley. On the other hand,
"How are you regimented in the other world?" would
have commended itself to Frederic W. H. Myers. It
is odd that Defoe, in his *Secrets of the Invisible World*,
roundly scolded Jeremy Taylor for these queries,
which he considered "needless and impertinent";
while that earnest believer in witches and goblins,
Increase Mather, was even more deeply scandalised
at Taylor's levity. We see in his questions to Taverner's tormentor, not exactly disbelief in the reality
of the apparition, but undoubtedly that hesitancy
which led him, in the *Dissuasion from Popery*, to
point out how dangerous credulity is, and how un-
likely it must be that God should give devils an
opportunity to "abuse the world with notices and
revelations of their own."

o

Another wild tale came before him in the adventure of a neatherd who was in his service at Portmore, and who was "amazed" by the apparition of an old woman, who pursued him for nearly nine months. In this case the ghost was also seen and followed by the neatherd's little dog. The old woman had buried twenty-eight shillings in her lifetime, and wished that this money, accompanied by an extremely tart reproof for his wicked and dissolute conduct, should go to one of her sons. At last, it would seem that the man consented to search for the money, which was buried under a hearth-stone "beyond the Bann Water," whereat the old woman was so rejoiced that she bade him lift her in his arms. He did so, and found her as light as a bag of feathers; whereupon she vanished forever in a most delicate music. Unfortunately, we are not told whether the twenty-eight shillings were discovered under the hearth-stone. In this story, also, both Jeremy Taylor and old Lady Conway took the acutest interest, but Alcock neglects to report the bishop's opinion on this case.

As soon as his clergy were settled in the diocese, Taylor collected them at Lisburn, and earnestly exhorted them on their personal and public deportment. His words betray his cordial desire for reconciliation with all classes of his flock. The incumbents, so embarrassingly deposited in unwelcome propinquity to obstructive parishioners, were above all things to "remember that discretion is the mistress of all graces." They were to discourage useless disputations; they were to devote themselves to the spirit of meekness, and to endeavour to gain over their flock "by the importunity of wise discourses." They were

to "strive to get the love of the congregation," yet
"let it not degenerate into popularity." As High
Church Anglicans they were to be careful to introduce no needless rites and gestures which would be
offensive to parishioners, but to keep to what was
required by the Church and established by law. They
were to be most particular not to incense the congregation by exasperating or scolding them, nor to
use irritating forms of language, "fantastical or schis-
matical terms." They must remember that they are
ministering among persons, who from ignorance or
prejudice are ready to be troublesome, and they must
give no occasion to disturbance. If the minister finds
in his congregation a contentious person, he is not to
dispute with him; he is to employ the man's zeal "in
something that is good, let it be pressed to fight against
sin." Nothing could be gentler or wiser than this advice, nothing more evangelical.

But Jeremy Taylor, while earnestly recommending
meekness, would not corrupt it into cowardice. The
clergy are not to forget that they are to rule and to
instruct, and that "he that receives from the people
what he shall teach them, is like a nurse that asks
of her child what physic she shall give him." They
are not to suffer the common people to prattle about
religious questions. They must see that no person
in their parishes is ignorant of the foundations of
faith, but they are forbidden to destroy their duty
by "unreasonable compliance with the humours" of
the flock. They are to check severely the common
fault of the sectaries, who were wont, it seems, after a
good dinner, to sit down and backbite their neighbours.
In short, the clergy of Down and Connor were to be

mild and yet firm, tender disciplinarians and constitutional rulers. It was a counsel of perfection, and little
time went by before Jeremy Taylor and George Rust,
who was his right-hand man, had a painful awakening
from their dream of a pacified and grateful Ulster.
For two years, from the summer of 1661 to that of
1663, all seems to have been tolerably calm in the
dioceses, and then a storm of Presbyterian recusancy
broke out again.

Jeremy Taylor became aware of what was going on
in the course of a visitation to the eastern part of
his diocese. The village of Killinchy, on Strangford
Lough, was the centre of a disaffection which was
caused by a visit paid to County Down by the noto-
rious adventurer, Colonel Thomas Blood. This man
had set no value upon the religious life, but he knew
how to play upon the sensibilities of fanatics. He
pretended to be a convinced Presbyterian, and he was
introduced to a knot of the ejected ministers by his
brother-in-law, of the name of Lecky. It is only fair,
however, to the Ulster Presbyterians to say that,
though they were in a state of great religious fermen-
tation, they would have none of Blood and his plot,
which was discovered in Dublin on the 22nd of May,
and prevented. Blood escaped to England, where he
had a chequered career as a rebel and a thief. But
all these events greatly disturbed opinion in Down
and Antrim, and led the government to some arbi-
trary acts. Taylor exaggerated the danger, and, on the
11th of June, wrote in great trepidation to the Duke
of Ormonde. He had discovered that John Drysdale,
one of the most formidable of the ejected ministers,
had returned from his exile in Scotland, and believed

that he was stirring up disaffection. He rashly arrested Drysdale, although "on no particular charge," and then asked the Duke for instructions. The Dublin government took prompt action; all the Presbyterian ministers who could be found in the counties of Antrim and Down were arrested, and imprisoned respectively at Carrickfergus and at Carlingford. After a considerable period of incarceration, as no charge could be proved against them, they were allowed to withdraw to Scotland, and the storm passed over.

In the new attitude which Jeremy Taylor adopted to his flock in 1663, it is possible that he was affected by the revival of zeal in England, of which the *Ichabod* of Ken, published in this very year, gives evidence. There was a strong feeling among youthful Anglicans that their elders were not showing a proper resentment against the "sad race of dissenters." Taylor may have been stirred by letters from England to show greater activity in silencing the disturbers of the peace of his diocese.

The executive took all the responsibility for these acts of violence, but it is impossible to overlook the fact that it was Jeremy Taylor who had appealed to the Duke for help, and that it was he who sketched the policy which the Dublin government carried out. He had appealed to the force of the law to remove the ministers, on the ground that as long as they remained in his diocese it would be "a perpetual seminary of schism and discontents," and he had roundly accused them of being "all more than consenting" to Blood's plot. In this last matter there is evidence that he was misinformed, but he has to bear the responsibility of the results of his grievous error.

In the midst of all these perturbations Archbishop
Bramhall died, on the 25th of June, and was succeeded
as Primate by Margetson, the Archbishop of Dublin,
a man of much milder temper, who inaugurated a
policy of conciliation in the northern provinces. I
think it probable that Jeremy Taylor not merely
acquiesced in this change, but positively welcomed
it. At Bramhall's funeral he preached a sermon
which, so willing are readers to find what they really
bring with them, has been mentioned as an instance of
Taylor's harsh and domineering temper, and of the
tormented conditions of his mind. I can only say that
I have searched this brilliant performance in vain for
any such evidence of bias. The *Funeral Sermon on
Archbishop Bramhall* is a composition in Taylor's most
careful manner; it is partly a rhapsody on the sure and
certain hope of resurrection, and partly a very skilful
and picturesque biography. The former section is curiously reminiscent of Sir Thomas Browne's then recent
Urn-Burial; the preacher "will not now insist upon
the story of the rising bones seen every year in Egypt,
nor the pretences of the chemists that they from the
ashes of flowers can reproduce the same beauties in
colour and figure," but he runs his parallels through
"night and day, the sun returning to the same point
of east, every change of species, the eagle renewing her
youth, and the snake her skin, the silkworm and the
swallows, winter and summer, the fall and spring," all
of them symbols and reflections of the glorious mystery of resurrection. We seem to be back again at
Golden Grove, so graceful is the imagery, so ethereal
the verbal music.

He turns from these contemplations to a portrait of

the great man whom they have met to bury.   He
dwells on his energy, his intellect, his virtue; he
insists, with indignant zeal, upon Bramhall's heroic
passion for the Church, and upon all that he was
called upon to suffer. He was driven into poverty and
exile by that wild storm "by which great Strafford
and Canterbury fell"; he returned to Ireland and to
honour at an hour so late that neither the King nor
Ormonde, "the King's great vicegerent," could reap
from his restoration the whole benefit they had anticipated. For Bramhall, with all his greatness, was then
already old and broken. "It is true he was in the
declension of his age and health. But his very ruins
were goodly. And they who saw the broken heaps of
Pompey's Theatre, and the crushed obelisks, and the
old face of beauteous Philenium, could not but admire
the disordered glories of such magnificent structures,
which were venerable in their very dust." In dilating
upon these qualities, it must have been a great temptation to Jeremy Taylor to denounce the Presbyterians,
whose tempestuous resistance had embittered Bramhall's last hours, and who pursued him beyond the grave
with their hatred. But not a word of anger escapes
the preacher; he does not so much as hint at any trouble
in the northern dioceses. The *Funeral Sermon on
Bramhall* is perfect in dignity and Christian reserve.
It appears to me that in later times it has been read too
little and too carelessly. It is the one piece of literature produced by Jeremy Taylor in Ireland which is
entirely worthy of his reputation as an artist. It is
the one effusion of those agitated years which shows
no decline from the lofty standard of his imagination
and intellect.

Jeremy Taylor's principal literary occupation, however, during the closing years of his life was the composition of an extremely lengthy *Dissuasion from Popery* addressed to the people of Ireland. He tells us that his brethren, the prelates of that country, set his task upon him, and that at first he was unwilling to adventure upon it. But, having once taken it up, he seemed incapable of dropping it. The viscous task adhered to his fingers, and one whose memory was so accurately stored with patristic instances needed but the very smallest intellectual stress to continue the disquisition almost indefinitely. A first — and surely a sufficient — instalment appeared in quarto in 1664; but Jeremy Taylor could not break through the glutinous chain of his animadversions, and proceeded to produce a Second Part, being a Vindication of the First, and further Reproof of Roman Error. This he had sent to press when he died, and it appeared in the autumn of 1667. Had his life been prolonged, we might now possess a Third Part, and a Fourth. This is the most languid and unreadable of Jeremy Taylor's writings. It is deformed by patronising remarks about "the poor deluded Irish," and in particular goes out of its way to attack the use and study of the Irish language, which Taylor thought barbarous and deforming, and wished to prohibit. His entire want of sympathy with the Celtic mind is illustrated by the agony of distress into which he is thrown by certain instances of its "miserable superstition and blindness." In every sentence we are conscious of the chasm which divided him from all sections of his flock, of what Matthew Arnold might call "the profound sense of estrangement" from them, "immense, incurable, fatal."

A recent learned writer on Jeremy Taylor has
called *A Dissuasion from Popery* "one of the most
interesting of his writings." The interest which Mr.
Alexander Gordon finds, must reside, I think, solely
in the definite statement of the deadlock existing
between the old religion of Ireland and the new, and
that is surely sufficiently contained in the dedication
to the Duke of Ormonde. The rest of this huge treatise we must not allow partiality for Taylor, or sympathy for his isolated position, to make us attempt to
admire. The antipathy it displays to the people of Ireland, its incurable Philistinism and ignorance of the
Celtic temperament, are not less disappointing because
they were shared by the majority of Englishmen in that
dreary period. And, as for Jeremy Taylor himself, so
far from thinking it "interesting" that he should spend
his last years almost exclusively in this multiplication of insulting diatribes against the ancestral religion
of his country, we should regard his labour mournfully
as a cardinal example of that objectless waste of energy
which Coleridge deplored as the worst of misfortunes: —

> " With lips unbrightened, wreathless brow, I stroll ;
> And would you learn the spells that drowse my soul ?
> Work without Hope draws nectar in a sieve,
> And Hope without an object cannot live."

Meanwhile the bishop was carrying on his campaign
against the Presbyterians of his diocese, and in this
he was aided by Sir Richard Kennedy, who acted in
Ulster as Judge of Assize. This lawyer, who was one
of the Barons of the Exchequer for Ireland, supported
Taylor in all his decisions, and in fanatical zeal even
went beyond the bishop's desires. Kennedy "infinitely

discountenanced and punished" the Nonconformists, and showed an intemperate activity in all the affairs of the Church. He went to such extremities that he had to be checked by orders from the Privy Council, which became alarmed at the reports of his severity. Among the gentry of Ulster, Lord Massereene was solitary in his efforts for peace and general indulgence, although others, such as Lady Ards and Lord Duncannon, interceded for personal friends of their own. By the early months of 1664 "the generality of the ministers of the North were either banished, imprisoned or driven into corners," but the anger of the populace was so great that the Duke of Ormonde found it wise to insist upon a slackening of the persecution. Jeremy Taylor "stormed at this vague favour for nonconformity," and encouraged Kennedy to pursue his work. But the Irish Primate had determined to be "civil to the brethren of Down," and Sir Richard Kennedy was felt to be so embarrassing to the government at Dublin, that he was urged to take occasion of the Lord Lieutenant's going over to England to accompany him, and not to return to Ireland. Jeremy Taylor found himself deserted and solitary.

On the 25th of May 1664 he wrote a pressing letter to his old friend Sheldon, now Archbishop of Canterbury, imploring to be translated to a less arduous see. Sheldon, it seems, had said that Jeremy Taylor himself was the only hindrance to his being removed to an English bishopric. Taylor protested that he could not conjecture what the Primate meant, but it is easy to see that his reputation for lack of suppleness and moderation had brought him into disgrace with the Court. No one appreciated his painful zeal, no one had wished him to be so stern and unbending to his clergy. His appeal to be solaced by a see in some other part of England or Ireland is pathetic. He writes: —

"I humbly desire that your grace will not wholly lay me aside, and cast off all thoughts of removing me. For no man shall with a greater diligence, humility and observance endeavour to make up his other disabilities than I shall. The case is so that the country does not agree with my health as it hath done formerly, till the last Michaelmas ; and if your grace be not willing I should die immaturely, I shall still hope you will bring me to or near yourself once more. But to God and to your grace I humbly submit the whole affair, humbly desiring a kind return to this letter, and the comfort of a little hope."

But Charles II. seems to have been told that the Presbyterians of Ulster " had been sufferers for the King," and Jeremy Taylor's last chance of promotion or even of translation passed away. He had pleased nobody ; his flock were persuaded that he was cruel and unjust, and the government regarded him as dangerous and embarrassing. For the rest of his life, as it was indicated to him again, he must make the best he could of Down and Connor. He buried himself in literature, and resigned himself to inevitable disappointment. From this time forward his animal spirits seem to have decayed. He had lost his hope, and with it went his energy. To this moment probably belongs the curious story preserved by Michael Lort, the antiquary, that Taylor desired his secretary to procure all the copies of his *Liberty of Prophesying* which could be found, and made a bonfire of them in the market-place of Dromore. It was not, indeed, like Jeremy Taylor to destroy one of his own works — although it may be noticed that *Liberty of Prophesying* is prac-

tically the only one of all his didactic books which
he did not include in the list of modern English
divinity drawn up at Graham's request in 1660 — but,
if the tale is true, it shows a repudiation of his early
theories of toleration which is melancholy in itself,
and not out of keeping with his distressing implaca-
bility as a bishop. The iron had entered into his soul,
and he was no longer the Jeremy Taylor whose patient
energy and active sympathy we have loved.

We hear little more of him in a public capacity.
He had a farm of forty acres at Magheralin, probably
the same which had been allotted to him through Sir
William Petty's offices when he first arrived in Ireland.
He devoted himself to this estate, and traces of his
beneficence remain in the whole district around it.
Traditions of him are said to be still extant in several of the surrounding villages, at Soldierstown, at
Derriaghy, at Magheragall, at Ballinderry. The places
where Jeremy Taylor is said to have "resided"
are numerous in the south-west of Antrim and the
north-west of Down. It must be remembered that
wherever a man of such prominence spent a single
night would easily be quoted in tradition as one of
his "residences." He probably lived chiefly at Hillsborough until April 1663, when Colonel Arthur Hill
died, an event which robbed the bishop of one of
his few close friends. He certainly still had a home
in or near Portmore, and when he left Hillsborough,
the house he had built in the Castle Street of Lisburn, opposite the doors of the cathedral, would be
his official residence. Everything seems to point to
a rapid decline in vitality during the last three years
of his disenchanted life. He had been an enthusiast

for liberty and love, but circumstances had forced him
to adopt the guise of a tyrant. He had lived for the
affection of his friends, and he found himself solitary
in a strange land. When the emotions of a sensitive
man cease to have an object, he soon pines away.

Jeremy Taylor's interest in architecture was noticeable, and as a builder he stamped his mark upon his
diocese. Unhappily, fire and the restorer have left
but few examples of his art for us to judge of its merit.
Until 1902, however, one specimen of Taylor as an
architect still survived intact. On a little eminence
south of the road which winds through the parish of
Ballinderry, in Antrim, four miles north of Moira, was
to be seen a deserted church, white-washed, with an
empty bell-cot, its chancel-end loaded with ivy, its only
remarkable feature being a row of circular-headed
mullion windows. This was the shell of that church
which Jeremy Taylor started building in 1665, and
to furnish which he dismantled of its oak fittings the
old chapel on Lough Beg, where he had officiated while
he was at Portmore. He brought slates for its roof
from Aberdovey, in Wales, and he seems to have spent a
good deal of money in making it a really pretty specimen
of belated Jacobean church architecture. It was in
danger of falling into complete ruin, when Mr. F. J.
Biggar, of Ardrie, Belfast, brought its rare interest to
the notice of Mrs. Walkington of Ballinderry, who had
it very carefully restored by Mr. W. J. Fennell, under
the inspection of Sir Thomas Drew. No new feature
was introduced, and the work was carried out with
the most conservative care. It was reconsecrated, in
October 1902, by Dr. Welland, the present Bishop of
Down, Connor and Dromore, and it is by far the most

interesting personal relic of Jeremy Taylor which
exists in Ireland.

There is little more to be recorded of his life.
About three years after the death of Arthur Hill, he
became engaged in a vexatious dispute with the
Colonel's son, Moses Hill, as to certain revenues from
the Castlereagh estate, which Jeremy Taylor had
enjoyed, and to which he said that he possessed a
right as bishop. In this Lord Conway agreed with
him, but Moses Hill protested that these had merely
been paid to Taylor as a matter of courtesy and
personal friendship. A lawsuit was the result, which
came before both Houses of the Irish Parliament; the
rents were sequestered and the suit was still pending
when the bishop died. This was a sad conclusion to
the long and harmonious friendship between Jeremy
Taylor and the house of Hillsborough. By this time
it is evident that Taylor was irritable with failing
strength. Until the autumn of 1663, however, Ireland
had suited his bodily health, and the conjecture that
he fell a victim to the supposed swampiness of his
dwelling rests on no evidence. As long as he resided
on the heights of Hillsborough he was in one of the
wholesomest spots in the county of Down. Later on,
in February 1666, when all Ireland, and England too,
was ringing with the strange, half-miraculous cures
which Valentine Greatrakes, "the Stroker," was effect-
ing by a kind of massage, Lord Conway wished Jeremy
Taylor to try whether the itinerant magician could
not recover him of his "distemper," but we know not
whether Taylor allowed Greatrakes to rub him, nor
what his distemper was.

His only surviving son, Charles, was now about

twenty-four years of age. He was consumptive, and
he died at the close of July 1667; on the 2nd of
August he was buried in London, in the church of
St. Margaret's, Westminster. On the following day
Jeremy Taylor, who had visited the bedside of a fever-
patient in Lisburn on the 24th of July, was taken ill,
and though he can hardly have heard of Charles's death,
the desperate condition of his only son must have been
known to him, and doubtless had its effect in depress-
ing his vital force. He lay sick for ten days in his
house at Lisburn, the disease being described as a
fever, and on the 13th of August 1667 he died, being
in all probability within a few days of completing his
fifty-fourth year. It is probable that he expected to
die, and perhaps made no effort to recover; he is said
to have wished to lie in his new church at Ballinderry,
but that was not yet consecrated. He added, therefore, and these are recorded as being his last words,
"Bury me at Dromore." His body, accordingly, was
taken on the 21st of August to the cathedral which
he had built in that little town. It was deposited in
the vault beneath the chancel, the funeral service being
performed by George Rust.

Such was the death of Jeremy Taylor, an event
which seems to have attracted no notice at all in
England and to have created little sensation even in
Ireland. There is something poignantly sad, and
almost ignominious, in this close to the life of a sensitive
man of genius. After a long experience of poverty and
glory, he had become wealthy at the sacrifice of almost
everything else which makes life desirable. We mourn
at the spectacle of the passing of one who had deserved
to be happy, and who had escaped happiness by so

small an interval, yet had escaped it wholly at the end;
who had manifestly striven to do his duty, yet with so
strange a want of tact in himself and of appositeness
in his surroundings, that the result in the eye of history bears a worse air even than dereliction would.

His Irish friends in the non-clerical world of
the diocese were all dead, or, like Lord Conway,
settled in England. No one seems to have cared to
preserve Jeremy Taylor's memory, which was not
recalled until, in 1827, Richard Mant, who was then
Bishop of Down and Connor, was roused by Heber's
reproaches to set up in the cathedral church of Lisburn
a tablet; this contained a lengthy and eulogistic
epitaph, claiming for Jeremy Taylor that his renown
was "second to that of none of the illustrious sons
whom the Anglican Church hath brought forth."
Meanwhile no stone was erected to mark the place of
Taylor's sepulture in Dromore Cathedral, and in 1670
the same fate befell the remains of his successor,
George Rust. There is a story that the bones of
these prelates were removed and scattered to make
room for a later Bishop of Dromore, and that when
Percy came to the diocese in 1782, he had them
collected and piously reinterred. This tradition has
been shown to rest on very slender evidence, but no
doubt the remains of the bishops did disappear. When
the Cathedral of Dromore was rebuilt in 1866, certain
bones were discovered lying in confusion. It was
taken for granted that these were the remains of the
bishops, and as one of the skulls was very much larger
than the rest, it was thought that it must belong to
the most intellectual of them. On this slender basis
of identification, it was buried in the choir, and a brass

proclaims the doubtful fact that here lie the bones of the celebrated Dr. Jeremy Taylor.[1]

A better authenticated and a far more durable monument to him was raised by his faithful companion and affectionate admirer, George Rust, Dean of Connor, the last and warmest of his friends. This took the shape of a funeral sermon, which is a composition beautiful in itself, and as a contribution to Taylor's biography simply invaluable. It was preached at Dromore on the 21st of August, and repeated in Dublin, at the funeral service, on the 3rd of September 1667. Rust, who is not known to have been personally acquainted with Taylor until the latter invited him over in 1661 to aid him in administering the diocese, must have obtained his information regarding earlier years mainly from the conversation of the bishop himself. Much that we know of Jeremy Taylor's life we owe entirely to Rust, and it is remarkable that on many points where Rust's statements have been distrusted or even rejected, further examination has proved him

---

[1] It is impossible, while recording the obscurity in which the bones of this glorious son of the English Church were permitted to lie in his Irish exile, not to recall the burning epitaph which Boileau wrote in 1694 for the unhonoured grave in Brussels of one whom Jeremy Taylor valued above all the other continental divines of his time : —

> Au pied de cet autel de structure grossière,
> Git sans pompe, enfermé dans une vile bière,
> Le plus savant mortel qui jamais ait écrit:
> ARNAULD, qui sur la grâce, instruit par Jésus-Christ,
> Combattant pour l'Église, a, dans l'Église même,
> Souffert plus d'un outrage et plus d'un anathême.

Not a word in this but is directly true of Taylor. But a reference to Pelagius follows, and Boileau's epitaph ceases to be applicable.

to be in the right. No life of Jeremy Taylor would
be complete without the words in which, closely and
successfully imitating the style of his subject, George
Rust paints him as he knew him : —

"This great prelate had the good humour of a gentleman, the
eloquence of an orator, the fancy of a poet, and the acuteness
of a schoolman, the profoundness of a philosopher, the wisdom
of a councillor, the sagacity of a prophet, the reason of an
angel, and the piety of a saint. He had devotion enough for
a cloister, learning enough for a university, and wit enough
for a college of virtuosi; and had his parts and endowments
been parcelled out among his poor clergymen that he left
behind him, it would perhaps have made one of the best
dioceses in the world. . . . He is fixed in an orb of glory, and
shines among his brethren-stars, that in their several ages gave
light to the world, and turned many souls unto righteousness ;
and we that are left behind, though we can never reach his
perfections, must study to imitate his virtues, that we may at
last come to sit at his feet in the mansions of glory."

CHAPTER VII

No one has asserted with more boldness than Coleridge the pre-eminence of Jeremy Taylor as a man of letters. He recognised his limitations as a theologian, as a thinker, but he insisted on his art as a writer, on the majesty of his "great and lovely mind." Coleridge placed Jeremy Taylor among the four principal masters of the English language in the august first half of the seventeenth century ; he "used to reckon Shakespeare and Bacon, Milton and Taylor, four-square, each against each." So luminous and penetrating are the words of Coleridge on Jeremy Taylor that we can but deeply regret the fact that they are casual and occasional, and are scattered here and there over the extent of his writings. "I believe such a complete man hardly shall we see again . . . such a miraculous combination of erudition, broad, deep, and omnigeneous, of logic subtle as well as acute, and as robust as agile . . . and of genuine imagination, with its streaming force unifying all at one moment like that of the setting sun when, through an interspace of blue sky no larger than itself, it emerges from the cloud to sink behind the mountain." How admirably just this is, with a felicity of expression worthy of the subject himself, only those can fully realise who turn to it from immersion in the alternate cloud and sunshine of Taylor's own marvellous writings.

It is remarkable that in this case of a genius comparable only with those of Shakespeare, Bacon, and Milton, we find ourselves confronted by a comparative neglect which requires some explanation. By the side of the fulness of exposition which has been given to the lives and writings of the three, the obscurity of the fourth is noticeable. But, in the first place, we must observe that the fame of Jeremy Taylor has been injured among general readers by the fact that he is a divine, and among divines by the fact that he is an artist. The theologian who is also a man of letters suffers from several disadvantages which criticism finds it easier to state than to remove. In the first place, like other professional and scientific authors, much of what he says, and indeed the important part of it, is definite statement into which the element of style cannot enter. The theologian, moreover, is obliged to use a great number of formulas and instances which are not his own, and with the form of which he dare not tamper. He is bound to have those words of Scripture, which never can be his own words, for ever on his lips. Before, therefore, we can reach the claim of the theologian to be an independent man of letters, we have to clear away a great deal which is said solely for purpose of instruction, and a great deal, too, which is beautiful, but which is not the substance of his own mind.

The theologian who devotes much attention to literary form is liable to suspicion of neglect of his primal duty. It is not to be questioned that Jeremy Taylor's astonishing brilliancy has damaged his influence as a pure divine. From the very first he was not a favourite with persons of a strenuous or Puritanical bent of mind, and could not be; because his pre-occupation with beauty was bound to be viewed with disfavour amongst those who felt that the humblest and baldest types of speech were sufficient to express exhortation, supplication, and contrition. But together with this too copious use of the ornaments of speech, there entered a certain forbidding sense of moral ineffectiveness, which, I believe, has done more than anything else to deprive Jeremy Taylor of the predominant rank which his art and his intellect demand for him. People are pleased that an author should be positive, definite, almost stubborn, while the personal attitude of Taylor to the faith is curiously irresolute. This strange condition is illuminated by a flash of intuition in one of Coleridge's letters (Nov. 3, 1814), where he says that the real "opinion" of Jeremy Taylor, as contrasted with the glorious rush of his eloquence, is "all weather-eaten, dim, useless, a ghost in marble." To illustrate this, by emphasising the contrast between Taylor's rigidity concerning the authority of the Church and his latitude in interpreting its Articles, would carry us into a field which must be carefully avoided in these pages; but this is an important element of what we may call discomfort in the attitude of the reader to his writings.

It is possible that the antagonisms and schisms within the English Church of the seventeenth century tended to depreciate the directness of its literary appeal. The result of always having to remember that offence might be taken by a large proportion of hearers must have been a constant disturbance of the

reflecting faculties of the preacher.   It was only a very
resolute character which could not be moved, either to
timidity or else to acrimony, by this sense of latent opposition.   The great English theologians of the seventeenth century — with one or two exceptions, among
whom Barrow is prominent — strike us as wanting in
that profound physical vitality, of which, on the other
side of the Channel, Bossuet and Fénelon were the
types.   But the absence of a powerful Nonconformity
is not to be overlooked as an immense aid to French
Catholic oratory.

We must now rapidly indicate Jeremy Taylor's position.   The theological literature of the seventeenth
century possesses a certain fixed character which to
the casual student of to-day is apt to seem monotonous
and to exclude individuality.   But when we begin to
examine it, the different tones of voice, the different
keys of colour, do not fail to assert themselves.   When
once we perceive the distinctions, we are even in danger
of exaggerating them.   We find ourselves wondering
that any one can ever have supposed that a page of
Pearson was like a page of Tillotson.   We close our
ears, and the tones of the voices seem entirely various, although in some cases it is difficult to define the
difference.   More than all, where the general texture
is bare and rough, the presence of brilliant ornament
becomes almost painfully insistent.   One can imagine
a reader, long steeped in Barrow, turning away,
dazzled and embarrassed, from the gorgeous embroi-
deries of Jeremy Taylor.   And, indeed, the first distinction a critic has to make in defining the literary
position of Taylor is founded on his own temperament.
We must cut him off at once from pure theologians

like Pearson and from pure grammarians like Wilkins. With those who cared for nothing but the pursuit of naked truth and with those whose pleasure lay in the logical sequence of language, he had no vital sympathy. He cared for truth mainly as a pathway to emotion, and for words only in the effect of their harmonious and telling arrangement.

The recognition of this fact greatly simplifies our task in seeking to define Taylor's position in English literature. His preoccupation with form, his magnificence in ornament, relegate him to a class in which but few of the divines of the seventeenth century make so much as an effort to accompany him. In the generation which preceded his, Donne and Joseph Hall had cultivated prose with studied care. In his own, Chillingworth possessed grace and rapidity of movement, Fuller, Henry More, and Cudworth were writers of great excellence. Without, however, in the slightest degree depreciating any of these admirable men, it is plain that in a serious comparison of them, as mere wielders of English, with Jeremy Taylor, all but Donne and Fuller withdraw into the second place at once. With the sonorous majesty of Donne's organ-sentences, the simpler and sweeter phrases of Taylor have some relation. Donne, with all his differences, is the one English preacher who seems to have left a mark on the style of Taylor. But the younger advanced beyond the elder in suppleness and variety, and even in splendour, as far as Pope advanced beyond Dryden in neatness and wit.

The only rival to Taylor is Fuller, who, if we examine closely, proves to be not so much a rival as a happy contrast. The present generation has no need to be reminded of the familiar genius of Fuller, garrulous and jocular, that "most appetising bundle of contradictions," as Professor Saintsbury has defined it. But we are perhaps in danger of overvaluing the prosaic picturesqueness of Fuller's active mind. He has been one of the most fortunate of English writers, indulged, excused, and petted by criticism, so that his very faults are found charming in the eyes of his doting admirers. Wit, as we know, was the sum and substance of his intellect, and it produced delightful effects, fresh and entertaining and boundlessly quaint. But to turn from it to the solemn art of Jeremy Taylor is to rise into a higher, if a rarer, atmosphere, to be nearer heaven, to come within earshot of a sublimer music. There is really no object in comparing two writers, the one so amiably mundane, the other so shining and seraphical.

In the foregoing chapters the writings of Jeremy Taylor have been briefly described in the order of their composition, as portions of the biographical narrative. This procedure seemed convenient for several reasons. In the first place, for its novelty, since hitherto the various critical examinations of his works, of which Heber's is the most elaborate, have invariably discussed them in groups, the devotional books together, the casuistical together. In the second place, to give each publication its historical position, with a brief statement of its character and contents, was to leave us free, in the general summing-up, to ignore altogether what is not essential. By resigning the biographical order, we should lose most important evidence as to the growth, maturity, and decline of Taylor's genius. By retaining it, we give ourselves an oppor-

tunity of examining that genius only when it reaches
its zenith of force and splendour. No writer is more
cruelly misjudged if we throw his writings into a sack,
and take from them samples at random. In his case
it is imperative that criticism should select before it
gives its final judgment.

The importance of approaching Jeremy Taylor when
he is at his best is obvious when we examine the habit
of his mind. No great author displays more curiously
the phenomenon of growth. The style of Taylor, in
all its happiest effects, is sensorial; he did not begin
to write well until he saw with distinctness. That is
the keynote of the genius of the man, it was one
which fed on pictures and impressions. This class of
intellect is always slow in growth, because it depends
on the accumulation of rich and complex reminiscences,
which have to be stored in the archives of the brain
before they can be brought out and used. A French
critic has noted that "un style d'images n'est jamais
précoce," and it is not until Jeremy Taylor is thirty
years of age that he begins to write what it gives a
sympathetic reader pleasure to follow. When he
arrived at Golden Grove, he had tasted the agitation
of life; he had acquired, in peril and unrest, the habit
of keen sensation. There followed complete repose of
brain and nerves, just at the moment when the precious
gift was sufficiently stored, when the mechanism was
completed, and needed but the touch of the operator;
when, in fact, Taylor had arrived at the condition
which Fénelon described when he said, "Mon cerveau
est comme un cabinet de peintures dont tous les
tableaux remueraient et se rangeraient au gré du
maître de la maison."

But if a style so concrete as Jeremy Taylor's does not belong to early life, neither is it characteristic of old age. We need therefore not be surprised to find the pictures fading early from the walls of Jeremy Taylor's brain. In fact, his visual faculty slackened soon, although the linguistic faculty survived to the end. But as we have seen that his genius was essentially sensorial, we can feel no surprise that when it ceased to be stirred by images and sensations, it ceased to be attractive. Our biographical method, then, has emphasised the rise and fall, and it has prepared us to make here the somewhat sweeping statement that all of Jeremy Taylor's work which is first-rate was published between 1650 and 1655; that outside this absolutely consummate group of his writings there is a less brilliant but still admirable group extending from *Liberty of Prophesying* in 1647 to *The Worthy Communicant* in 1660; and that the rest of his works, with very slight exceptions, may be dismissed from literary criticism altogether.

In examining the books in which the style of Jeremy Taylor is seen at his best, we notice first, as their prominently distinguishing feature, their beauty. Taylor is not afraid of bold and brilliant effects, he is even ready to court them. His preoccupation with beauty, not in any secondary or suggested form, but in the most gorgeous scarlet and gold of fancy, and accompanied by flutes and hautboys of calculated cadence, distinguishes him at once from all his fellows. There is nobody, except Sir Thomas Browne, in the hundred years of English prose between the Euphuists and Shaftesbury, who can be mentioned in the same breath with Taylor for this richness of imaginative ornament.

But he is lifted above all prose-writers of the seventeenth century, even above Browne, by his simplicity, his natural air. He says things which are audacious enough for Shakespeare, and gorgeous enough for Ruskin, but he says them in perfect naturalness. It is in this that his powerful charm resides, and it is to do Jeremy Taylor the cruelest injury to confound his manner with that of Lyly or the later disciples of Marini. When the author of *Euphues* tells us that "the precious stone autharsitis, being thrown into the fire, looketh black and half dead, but being cast into the water, glisteneth like the sunbeams," he is introducing into his narrative a piece of dead ornament to dazzle us. He knows absolutely nothing about "the precious stone autharsitis," but he thinks that it will impress the reader. But when Taylor says, "A brother if he be worthy is the readiest and nearest to be a friend, but till he be so, he is but the twilight of the day, and but the blossom to the fairest fruit of paradise," the illustration is apt and just, and, as it were, an inevitable aid in the expansion of the thought.

It is in this extraordinary vitality and organic growth of his metaphors that Taylor is really, what he is so often called, "the Shakespeare of English prose."[1] His visual memory was a well of images into which his fancy was incessantly descending, to return brimful of new combinations and illustrations. His taste was very pure, and for all his florid ornament, there is perhaps no writer of the time whose metaphors seem

[1] This epithet was first applied to Jeremy Taylor not, as is commonly supposed, by Gray, but by William Mason, the biographer of Gray. Mason is not rich enough to bear being robbed of the happiest of all his phrases.

to us less forced, or less incongruous. Certain primal
elements are extremely fascinating to him; of the
attraction to him of effects of light and of water we
shall presently speak. But it is to be noted that all
his inductions from natural phenomena have that
fervour which is needful to give this species of ornament real value. When his prose is richest, when it
leaps with greatest daring from image to image, it
always preserves "that entire, unsuspecting, unfear-
ing, childlike profusion of feeling" which Coleridge so
accurately noted as its leading characteristic. Whether
Taylor illustrates his meaning by the roughness of a
sour grape upon the palate or by the penetration of
a bee's sting in the finger, whether it is the unskilful
navigation of lads in a boat rocked upon the tide which
inflames his reflection, or the flutter of leaf-gold under
the breath of an artisan, it is always his sincere and
vivid emotion which shines forth below the image.

He writes with extraordinary happiness about light
and water. Nothing would be easier, if we had the
space, than to produce an anthology from his works,
and confine it scrupulously to those two themes. He
is quick, beyond any other man then living, in observing the effects of flashes of lightning in a dark room,
of beams of the sun breaking through the vapour of
rain, and divided by it into sheaves of rays, of wax
candles burning in the sunshine, of different qualities
of beautiful radiance in the eyes of a woman, of a
child, of a hawk. Light escaping from, or dispersed
by, or streaming through cloud, is incessantly interesting to him. But perhaps it is in all the forms
of water that he most delights, water bubbling up
through turf, or standing in drops on stone, or racing

down a country lane; the motion and whisper of little wandering rivulets; the "purls of a spring that sweats through the bottom of a bank, and intenerates the stubborn pavement till it hath made it fit for the impression of a child's foot." He seems to have been for ever watching the eddies of the Towey and the windings and bubblings of its tributaries, and the music of those erratic waters passed into his speech.

Like all his contemporaries, he examines nature with near-sighted eyes. The mountains of Wales, even that panorama which was seventy years later to fill the first landscape-painters and descriptive poets with rapture, are as unseen by Jeremy Taylor as the tors of Dartmoor are by Herrick. The author of the *Eniautos* has no word about the great outlines of the country-side, but in the articulations of an insect or the softness of the stalk of a violet nothing escapes him. He notes the darting movement of a mouse over his shoe; the elasticity and the tenderness of the young ringed tendrils of a vine; the metamorphosis of the silkworm-moth, that "casting its pearly seeds for the young to breed, leaveth its silk for man, and dieth all white and winged in the shape of a flying creature, — so is the progress of souls." For glow-worms, grass-hoppers, butterflies, and the little dark ephemera that cling to walls, he has a searching eye, and fixes on their characteristic phenomena. He notes all the vicissitudes in the life of an apple-tree, its gum, its sterile branches, the fragility of its blossoms. He is acutely sensitive to odours, and finds metaphors for his use in the volatility of balsam and nard and camphor, in the keenness of their attack upon the brain, in the curious association of perfumes with events and places. Ugly things take their rank, too, in the records of his memory; he stores up for illustration the icy stiffness of a dead man's fingers, the intolerable beating of a watch in the darkness, the disagreeable sound of gravel on a wheel. These instances of Jeremy Taylor's sensorial style might be prolonged almost indefinitely. With the solitary exception of Shakespeare, there is no writer in all our early literature who has made so fresh and copious and effective a use of metaphor taken directly from the observation of natural objects.

With this pre-occupation with phenomena, Jeremy Taylor combines a habit which we may hastily fancy to be antagonistic to it. There is no great writer, except Burton, who introduces into his English prose such incessant citation of or reference to the classics as Taylor does. But this custom does not often impair the freshness of his outlook upon life. It has always to be remembered that the imitation of the ancients was a form of originality in the seventeenth century; it enabled writers to be daring and yet safe. The method of use of the classical poets by a master of such genius as Jeremy Taylor was either that he said, with their help, but by no means in literal translation, what had not been said in English before; or else that he transposed the style of the ancients into another style, entirely distinct from theirs and personal to himself. Even Democritus Junior had taken that view of the independence of his industry — "as a good housewife out of divers fleeces weaves one piece of cloth, a bee gathers wax and honey out of many flowers, and makes a new bundle of all, I have laboriously collected this cento out of divers writers."

Taylor, however, does not dream of collecting such a cento, or of illustrating the ancient authors in any way; he forces them to illustrate him, generally very much indeed against their will, with haughty disregard of their intention. He is impregnated with the odour of some of the ancients, and he uses them, as we saw that he used the natural phenomena around him, as a well of images into which he dips his imagination.

Sometimes he fuses the fragment of Latin poetry into his prose without much alteration, as when, in *The Worthy Communicant*, we find, " What if you empty all the Mævanian valleys, and drive the fat lambs in flocks unto the altars ? What if you sacrifice a herd of white bulls from Clitumnus ? " because Statius had said : —

> " Nec si vacuet Mævania valles,
> Aut præstent niveos Clitumna novalia tauros,
> Sufficiam."

But he does not prefer this metallic method, and much more often he uses the classical quotation or reference merely as an ingredient, sometimes faintly suggested, sometimes left so obvious as to give its unction to the passage while yet defying definite paraphrase, as in *A Discourse of Friendship*, where an exquisitely graceful chain of reflections is based upon the

> " Ut præstem Pyladen, aliquis mihi præstet Oresten "

of Martial without a single word being borrowed from the epigrammatist, although the sense of the Latin is unmistakably dissolved into the English. It must be confessed that the latter method, employing the

ancients as a *gradus* of experiences, is by far the
more fortunate, and that the English style of Jeremy
Taylor is usually spoiled when he attempts the crude
transference of classic poetry into his own prose.

It is impossible not to wonder whether the profusion of Latin and Greek quotation in Jeremy Taylor's
sermons was appreciated by his auditors.   There can be
no doubt that it was admired ; yet even in that learned
age Burton had refrained from Greek, because this
language was unfamiliar to the public.   Taylor almost
invariably translates, at once, any passage which he
has quoted in the original, and it is not impossible
that the translation only was spoken, and the Greek
added when the sermon was published.   We know,
indeed, that pulpit-learning was in fashion, and that
there were people who, as Earle tells us in his *Micro-
cosmographie*, came to sermons only that they might
approve of the references to Tacitus and Seneca.   But
Taylor would not have encouraged mere pretentious
pedantry.   He doubtless considered, in the spirit of
the then dying Renaissance, that there was no safety
for literature, no solid basis for taste, but in dependence on the classics.   There is scarcely a single passage in his variegated writings in which he admits
consciousness of the existence of a modern author who
does not write in Latin.   This scorn of vernacular
literature is very paradoxical in a man who laboured
to write English with the most exquisite art and
delicacy.   It has already been observed that Taylor
had a peculiar cult for Prudentius, whom he is never
tired of quoting.   The Spanish poet would have for him
the double charm of belonging to the classical tradition, and yet of being Christian.   Perhaps something

in the career of Prudentius, a courtier and soldier,
who withdrew from the world into a literary seclusion,
may have reminded him of his own adventures. But
an indifference to critical distinctions seems involved
in the habitual reference to Cicero and to Lactantius,
to Virgil and to Prudentius, as if these were names
of precisely the same intrinsic value. It must be confessed, too, that it is annoying to feel that an orator
who found such acute enjoyment in the verse of
Æschylus was prevented by a prejudice from finding
it also in that of Shakespeare.

It is perhaps connected with his critical insensibility,
if it may so be called, that Jeremy Taylor, although
he devotes so much attention to the classics, is singularly little affected by their principles in his grammar.
His syntax is not founded, as is that of Sir Thomas
Browne, on an obstinate preference for the Latin
system. Taylor's ideas of grammatical composition
were whimsical in the highest degree, and in the course
of one of his long breathless sentences he will shift
his tenses and link his noun to some neighbouring
verb that shrinks, intimidated, from the unwelcome
conjunction. The laxity of Taylor's grammar, so
widely opposed to the elegant correctness of Dryden
and Cowley, his younger contemporaries, has, however,
not scandalised all his critics. Coleridge boldly defends
it, and declares that if the syntax of Taylor is occasionally eccentric, it involves no difficulties of compre-
hension. But even if we admit that "a man long
accustomed to silent and solitary meditation is apt
to lose or lessen the talent of communicating his
thoughts with grace and perspicuity," the excuse
hardly touches the question of Jeremy Taylor's gram-

Q

mar; since he is not accused of lack of grace, nor of
any want of perspicuity save what directly arises from
the fault which Mr. Saintsbury notes, that "he breaks
Priscian's head with the calmest unconcern."

The long sentences of Jeremy Taylor have, on the
other hand, been unjustly blamed. In his finest
writings the volume of the "stately march and difficult evolutions" is mainly a matter of punctuation.
Taylor's printers had an objection to the full stop, and
they covered the page with commas and semicolons
when a point was what they should have used. To
repunctuate Taylor would be an act of real editorial
kindness, and no author suffers more than he from that
affectation which loves to reproduce in a modern book
the irrational errors of an old printer. Another cause
of the apparent length of Taylor's sentences is the
rhetorical "and" with which he loves to link the independent sequents of them. It is a trick of oratory;
by his conjunctions he thinks to hold the attention of
the listener. If we leave out the needless "ands,"
mere inspirations of the breath, in reading, we find
some of his longest sentences broken up into intelligible and completely effective modern prose. He was
a conscious rhetorician, and in his most studied passages it is rather to the ear than to the eye that he
appeals. His use of "Stay!" and "What?" and
"Well!" as modes of opening a sentence, or cluster
of sentences, is notable in this connection.

The main quality of Taylor's style is its splendour,
and the fact that he is extraordinarily florid and ornate
has led to his being charged with artificiality. But
although, as Coleridge has noted, Taylor's discursive
intellect sometimes "dazzle-darkened his intuition,"

making him desire to say, at the same moment, and in prodigious language, more things than a human brain can endure in concert, his actual writing was rarely turgid or difficult. In that age great magnificence of imagery was easily excused for robing itself in pomposity of language. The *Cypress Grove* of William Drummond had introduced a habit of excessively rich and sonorous prose, which developed, when it was abused, into mere tumidity. Taylor's meditations upon death are related, like those of Burnet, Browne, and Leighton, to this habit of superlative grandiloquence. But he never allows himself to lose his balance. He redeems his emotion, at the most critical moment, by some phrase of extreme simplicity. In this tact of his, and in the command he never loses over his wealth of metaphors and chains of sonorous polysyllables, he again constantly reminds the reader of Shakespeare. At the close of one of his most perilous outbursts of mortuary splendour, his voice drops into a whisper: "She lived as we all should live, and she died — as I fain would die." These sudden, pathetic felicities are always at his command. They greatly add to the charm of one of the most elaborate of the sections of his work, his beautifully constructed biographical funeral sermons.

As a rule the vocabulary of Taylor is easy and modern. He clung less than most of his contemporaries to obsolete forms of speech, and his genius naturally predisposed him to an easy elegance in the choice of words. By the side of Milton, for instance, whose curious vocabulary in prose seems sometimes almost affected in its oddity, Taylor appears of a newer fashion, less eccentric, anxious to avoid what is grotesque. Taylor would not have been a child of the late Renaissance, if he had not justified his right to impose certain words on the vernacular. He has a few favourite locutions of his own, and the close reader of his books soon comes to recognise *lipothymy, eutaxy, dyscrasy, coloquintida,* and *discalceate* as old friends. All these have preserved their place in our dictionaries, and although none of them is in common use to-day, they must pass as English words. We do not find in the pages of Jeremy Taylor those new-fangled terms of pedantry which, all unacceptable and unaccepted, were urged in vain by his contemporaries on the unwilling English grammarians, and dropped immediately into oblivion.

THE END

INDEX